Forest Seed Technology
Basic Concepts

NIPA® GENX ELECTRONIC RESOURCES & SOLUTIONS P. LTD.
New Delhi-110 034

About the Authors

Prof. T. H. Masoodi is presently working as Registrar Sheri-Kashmir University of Agricultural Sciences and technology of Kashmir, SKUAS-K) Shalimar. Prior to this Prof. Masoodi has served in the various capacities like Dean Faculty of Forestry, Director Research, Associate Director Research Leh and Head department of forestry SKUAST-Kashmir. Having more than thirty years of experience in the field of forestry, and doctoral degree from FRI, Dehradun, Prof. Masoodi has been associated with academics, research and extension work with more than 100 publications of international repute in national and international journals and has guided more than 15 students and masters and doctorate level. He has handled around 20 external funded projects as PI/Co-PI and has been member of various state/national level agencies. Prof. Masoodi has been instrumental in conducting number of trainings and bringing technology from lab to land in leh-Ladakh for the welfare of the farming community.

Dr. Parvez A. Sofi is working as Professor and Head in the Division of Forest Products and Utilization, Faculty of Forestry, Sher-e-Kashmir University of Agricultural Sciences and Technology of Kashmir, India. Dr. Sofi has completed his Ph.D Forestry from Dr. Y. S. Parmar University of Horticulture and Forestry, Nauni, Solan (H.P). Dr. Sofi is a motivating teacher and scientist driven to inspire students to pursue academic and personal excellence with over 19 yrs of experience in teaching, research and extension in the field of Forestry. He has an exceptional track record of research success with more than 100 publications of National and International repute. Besides Dr. Sofi has developed many technologies and value added herbal products in medicinal and aromatic plants. He is pioneer in establishing MAP based revenue generation models at the Faculty of Forestry SKUAST-Kashmir. Dr. Sofi is the peer reviewer of International Journal of Agricultural Sciences (IJAS), besides member of various national and international organizations. He is also member of various statutory bodies of the University. Dr. Sofi has guided dozens of M.Sc and Ph.D students and is also Nodal officer of All India Coordinated Research Project on Medicinal and Aromatic Plants and National Bamboo Mission. Dr. Sofi has handled number of externally funded projects and is also the author of many books and book chapters.

Dr. Nazir A. Pala, Assistant Professor in the Division of Silviculture & Agroforestry, Faculty of Forestry, SKUAST-Kashmir has more than ten years of experience in teaching and research. Prior to this Dr. Pala has the experience of working at UBKV, West Bengal, Himgiri Zee University Dehradun, Dolphin Institute, Dehradun, TERI, New Delhi, EIA consultant at NTPC, Govt. of India. Dr. Pala has been involved in handling several external funded projects and has more than 200 research publication and 04 books of national and international repute to his credit. Dr. Pala is the member of several international environmental organizations apart from being on the editorial board/reviewer of number of international journals.

Forest Seed Technology
Basic Concepts

T. H. Masoodi
Registrar
Sheri-Kashmir University of Agricultural Sciences
and Technology of Kashmir
Shalimar, Kashmir
Jammu and Kashmir, India

P. A. Sofi
Professor and Head
Division of Forest Products and Utilization
Sher-e-Kashmir University of Agricultural Sciences
and Technology of Kashmir
Shalimar, Kashmir
Jammu and Kashmir, India

Nazir A. Pala
Assistant Professor
Division of Silviculture & Agroforestry
Faculty of Forestry
Sheri-Kashmir University of Agricultural Sciences
and Technology of Kashmir
Shalimar, Kashmir
Jammu and Kashmir, India

NIPA® GENX ELECTRONIC RESOURCES & SOLUTIONS P. LTD.
New Delhi-110 034

NIPA® GENX ELECTRONIC RESOURCES & SOLUTIONS P. LTD.

101,103, Vikas Surya Plaza, CU Block
L.S.C. Market, Pitam Pura, New Delhi-110 034
Ph : +91-11-43860225, Mob.: +91 9717133558, 9540816132
E-mail: newindiapublishingagency@gmail.com
Website: www.nipaersources.com

Print ISBN: 978-93-58875-55-3
ebook ISBN: 978-93-58872-53-8

Composed and Designed by NIPA®.

Preface

Seed is the primary input for any productive forestry and afforestation programme. The global communities around the world are looking for increasing forest tree cover for both environmental amelioration and livelihood purpose. These both issues are possible when we have quality seed and planting material. Larg quantities of seeds are needed every year to raise the nursery stock for propagating the desired plant material. Hence a plentiful supply of quality seed is therefore one of the prerequisites to make such activities successful. Seeds are also one of the important sources of germplasm conservation and methods of harvesting, collection, storage and other properties need to assessed on scientific grounds. Seed viability varies from species to species and is affected by various locality factors and physiology. Seed testing and certification is important for quality seed production and storage. In view of the increasing demand for quality seed production of various afforestation programmes and the numerous challenges in various seed processing steps, the present book is very important for the students to learn the basic concepts of seed science. The present volume deals with the basic concepts of forest seed science including testing.

T. H. Masoodi
P. A. Sofi
Nazir A. Pala

Contents

1

Seed Biology

Seed bearing plants

Seed-bearing plants are broadly categorized in two major types: the gymnosperms and the angiosperms which are together grouped in Division Spermatophyta in the older system of classification for the plant kingdom. Consequently, seed plants are presently classified into multiple phyla. Still, for the purpose of learning basic concepts, it is convenient to group plants informally as spermatophytes (*sperm* "seed" + *phyte* "plant"). The spermatophytes are the most complex and evolutionarily advanced plants. Unlike ferns and bryophytes which reproduce and disperse by unicellular spores, spermatophytes reproduce and disperse by means of multi-cellular seeds which consist a protective seed coat surrounding an embryonic sporophyte and its food supply. This group of seed plants exhibits an alternation of generations in which the sporophyte is dominant. Furthermore, the gametophyte is microscopic and heterosporous with the latter term meaning that these seed plants produce two types of spores: microspores and megaspores that give rise to separate male gametophytes (micro-gametophytes) and female gametophytes (mega-gametophytes) respectively. The megaspore is never released from the sporangium; thus, the female gametophyte develops within the sporangium while being still attached to the sporophyte.

Spermatophytes share the following characteristics

- Dominant sporophyte
- Vascular tissues present (*tracheophytes*)
- Sporophyte body complex: true roots and stem present
- Leaf: megaphyll
- Extremely reduced endosporic heterosporous gametophyte
- Pollination precedes fertilization eliminating the need for free-water for fertilization
- Reproduction and dispersal by seeds

The Division Spermatophyta is further divided into two subdivisions: the Angiosperms and the Gymnosperms. The subdivision Angiosperm '(Gr. angio, a vessel + Gr. sperma, seed) refers to a set of plants with a special structure of megasporophyll which encloses the ovule that in turn contains a developing seed in a pistil or carpel. The Angiospermae makes up an extremely diverse group consisting of more than 3,000,000 species grouped in about 12,000 genera all of which produce true flowers and the ovules that are totally enclosed within the ovary.

Dicotyledonous forms the largest class of woody plants represented by many families, the prominent being Acanthaceae, Aceraceae, Cactaceae, Crassulaceae, Euphorbiaceae, Fabaceae, Fagaceae, Hydrangeaceae, Pittosporaceae, Platanaceae, Rosaceae, Salicaceae, Sapindaceae, Saxifragaceae, Ulmaceae, Vitaceae etc. The gymnosperms are a group of seed-producing plants that includes conifers, cycads, ginkgo, and gnetales. The reproductive structures of gymnosperms (Gr. gymnos, naked + sperma, seed) are called strobili. The microsporangia and megasporangia are produced in separate cones, even though both are commonly found on the same sporophyte or tree. The gymnosperms are represented by four major subgroups (Bold *et al.,* 1980):

- Phylum Cycadophyta -- the cycads;
- Phylum Coniferophyta -- the conifers
- Phylum Ginkgophyta -- ginkgo
- Phylum Gnetophyta --the gnetophytes

Phylum (from the Greek *kykas*, "a sago palm") **Cycadophyta** -- Very important plant group during the Triassic period, which occurred approximately 250 million years ago. They appeared in the Carboniferous and became very abundant during the Mesozoic (Jurassic to Cretaceous) followed by a decline through the Tertiary. Curiously, Nagalingum *et al.* (2011) found through fossil-calibrated molecular phylogenies that the cycads experienced a brief renaissance during the Miocene followed by a decline to the present level of diversity (~300 species) such that the divergence of all living species is no older than 12 million years old. The few survivors today are dioecious producing microsporangial (male) cones and ovulate (female) cones at the terminal end of the trunk (which is unbranched). They are rarely dominant in those environments where they occur.

Phylum Coniferophyta (cone bearers)- Coniferophyta (ko-ni-fe-ra-fa-ta) is made from two Latin and one Greek root that mean cone (*conus*); bear (*fero*); plant (phyto -φυτο). Their similarities to the progymnosperms have led authors like Pearson (1995) to place them near the root of the gymnosperm phylogeny. Crane (1996) advocated that conifers emerging with the gink gophytes and cycads are sisters to the gnetophyte-flowering plant clade. Chaw *et al.* (2000) and Bowe (2000) present similar analyses based on multiple genes (3 genomes: nuclear, mitochondrial, and chloroplast) in which *Ginkgo* is a sister to the gnetophyte-conifer clade. Other analyses (Zhong *et al.* 2010, Zhong *et al.* 2011) suggest the gne-cup hypothesis in which the gnetophytes are sisters to the Cupressopsida clade of the conifers. Other analyses (Ran *et al.* 2010) show that the gnetophytes are sisters to the conifers or sisters to all living seed-bearing plants (Rai *et al.* 2008). Fossil and morphological analyses associate the gnetophytes with the flowering plants (Hilton and Bateman 2006, Doyle 2006).

Conifers are represented by four prominent families: Pinaceae, Taxodiaceae, Cupressaceae and Taxaceae. Comprising about 550 species, it is by far the largest, most abundant and species-rich group of the plants. The reproductive pattern of conifers has several important strategies that are adapted for survival in unfavorable environments. Firstly, the plants are monoecious (pollen cones and ovulate cones borne together on the same individual) usually pollinated by the wind. The gametophyte (haploid state) is not dependent on external moisture. The non-motile sperm are enclosed within the pollen grain and are delivered to an egg during the corresponding growth of the pollen tube. Therefore, the fertilization does not require external agencies. Unlike other gymnosperms, in which pollination, fertilization, and seed maturation occur within the same year, the pines have an extended reproductive cycle of 14-20 months. Secondly, the female gametophyte is protected from drying out by remaining within the ovule, which is still attached to the cone. Thirdly, the immature sporophyte (diploid state) is dispersed by the seed, within which it is enclosed. The Typical examples of conifers include *Abies, Cedrus, Larix, Pinus, Pseudolarix, Pseudotsuga, Tsuga, Picea, Cryptomeria, Cunninghamia, Metasequoia, Sciadopitys, Sequoia, Sequoiadendron, Taxodium, Callitris, Chamaecyparis, Cupressus, Juniperus, Thuja, Agathis, Araucaria, Aucarioxylon, Podocarpus, Cephalotaxus and Taxus.*

Phylum Ginkgophyta - The ginkgophytes are represented by a single extant species the *Ginkgo biloba* which is exclusively dioecious and deciduous. It is the oldest known genus (and species) of living trees. That is why like the cycads, ginkgo has a fossil history that extends back to the Paleozoic and a flowering of abundance during the Mesozoic. The Introduction of this species to the American continent and Europe as an ornamental tree is credited with saving it from extinction. Vegetatively; the ginkgophytes more closely resemble conifers with woody monopodial growth, spur shoots, long shoots, and conifer-like roots. The fan-like leaves of *Ginkgo* have a fern-like dichotomously branched veination.

Phylum Gnetophyta - Gnetophyta (ne-TA-fa-ta) is derived from the Moluccan Malay word Gamemu and plant (phyto -φυτο). This group is reduced to three far-flung and remarkably different genera (each genus in its own order). They have very few vegetative synapomorphies except decussate leaves. However, the similarities in reproductive structures serve to unite the taxa. All are dioecious and both the ovulate and staminate strobili are compound. They have distinctive ovules with elongate tubular micropyles and extra integuments. The similarities with flowering plants include the occurrence of vessels in the xylem, double fertilization, net-veining in the leaves of *Gnetum*, and dicotyledonous embryos. Despite of this, the other compelling evidence; mainly molecular, places them as a sister group to the Pinales and squarely within the Coniferophyta (Doyle 2006).

Seed and fruit development

It is mainly concerned with the synthesis and storage of carbohydrate, protein, and oil to supply nutrients to the germinating seedling prior to emergence. Seed development occurs in several stages: rapid cell division, seed fill, and desiccation with each stage being species-specific and environmentally influenced. The seed is produced through a complex cycle of biological events, from the initiation of the flowering buds to their development, pollination, fertilization and finally seed formation.

Gymnosperms

Gymnosperms are all fruitless seed plants characterized by the production of naked seeds. Estimates from fossil records indicate that gymnosperms must have evolved approximately 300 million years ago from non-seed producing ancestors of the extinct division of Progymnospermophyta, which were fern-like in appearance. Gymnosperms, like angiosperms (the flowering plants), differ from seedless plants (like mosses and ferns) in not requiring water for sperm to swim to reach the egg. This means that the movement of pollen (male gamete) to ovule (female gamete) in seed plants relies on airborne transport, not water transport. The specialized characteristics in gymnosperms are:

i. In gymnosperms, pollen is found (located) in stamen-like structures called strobili (various types of cones). (Strobilus = singular).

ii. Junipers have strobili- fleshy cones, with a berry-like appearance. The fleshy scales are fused together and completely envelop the seed. Cones at maturity may be orange, red, brown, purple, or black, depending on the species. Birds eat the cones and swallow the seeds, which are then dispersed in their droppings.

iii. The pollen grains of Pinus and several other genera have bladder-like wings.

iv. Each male of a pine tree cone annually releases an estimated 1-2 million pollen grains.

v. They lack the folded, marginally-sealed carpels that characterize the flowering plants.

vi. The pollen-receptive structures are the ovules rather than the stigmatic portion of the carpels. Most gymnosperms lack vessels in their xylem (unlike flowering plants which have both vessels and tracheids), except for the gnetophytes, which have vessels.

Development of reproductive structures

Formation of Microsporangiate strobili (male cone), microsporophylls and microsporangia

Microsporangiate cones (in the vernacular, male cones; more technically, strobili) are smaller, structurally less complex, and more ephemeral than their megasporangiate counterparts. The pollen cone develops during early spring when a pair of microsporangia is borne on the abaxial (lower) surface of each microsporophyll which are arranged spirally along a specialized axis and; as a unit, constitute the microsporangiate strobilus. They are usually produced either singly or in clusters near the tips of lower younger branches. The mature pollen cones are always small, commonly less that 1" long, whereas the ovulate cones are large, measuring up to 2 ft long in the sugar pine. A very small proportion of these pollen grains reach the female cones where the microgametophyte will commence its development and form the gametes (non-motile sperm). After the release of pollen grains, the pollen cone dries up and falls off. The male cone (microstrobilus or pollen cone) is structurally similar across all conifers, differing only in small ways (mostly in scale arrangement) from species to species.

Megasporangiate strobili (female cone), ovuliferous scales, bracts, and ovules

Megasporangiate strobili (female cones) also known as ovulate cones are more complicated and consist of an ovoid, cylindrical, or spherical cluster of sporophylls (cone scales subtended by a scale-like bract) arranged around a central woody axis. They are much larger, structurally more complex, and persist longer on their parental sporophytes than do microsporangiate strobili (male cones). Each ovuliferous scale has two reduced megasporophylls (a leaf bearing a megasporangium). The megasporangium, or nucleus is contained within the ovuliferous scale of the parental sporophyte. Except for a small pore that faces the central axis of the cone (the micropyle), the megasporangium itself is completely covered by a thick layer of parental sporophytic tissue called the integument. This integument will eventually harden into the strong seed coat that will enclose the embryonic new sporophytic generation when it is dispersed from the parent tree. The integument and its contents (megasporangium, megagametophyte, and/or egg) comprise the ovule. Pine seeds are usually dispersed during autumn when the scales of ovulate cones separate. Cones of some pines do not open so gracefully or easily: these cones often require a fire to cause them to open and release their seeds (serotiny). The cones of some pines explode like popcorn when heated.

Pollination

In the spring when pollination occurs, young female cones will elongate slightly, such that the ovuliferous scales separate to a small extent. Pollen borne on the wind comes to rest between these open scales, and some may shift down toward the central axis of the cone. At this time a droplet of sticky fluid is formed near the micropyle, and as it dries out, any pollen in it will be drawn through the micropyle and onto the surface of the megasporangium. After pollination, the ovuliferous scales again are tightly enclosed until the seeds are dispersed. The pollination takes place as follows:

1. Ovules (immature seeds) develop on the surface of megasporophyll. They are not enclosed in an ovary.
2. Sporophylls are usually borne in clusters known as strobili ("cones").
3. A megasporangium (nucleus) formed on a fertile leaf (megasporophyll) is surrounded by an integument.
4. The megasporangium contains one megasporocyte that undergoes meiosis to produce four (4) megaspores, three (3) of which degenerate to give one functional megaspore.
5. The haploid megaspore divides by mitosis to produce a multicellular megagametophyte which forms two (2) archegonia each containing an egg.

Seed Formation in gymnosperms

Phylum Coniferophyta - The conifers

Seed production is an adaptation of great significance for the survival and dispersal of plants. In fact, this was part of the competitive advantage that allowed the gymnosperms to supersede the other vascular plants as the dominant type of vegetation on land. Only the later evolution of flower and fruit allowed another group of seed plants (the angiosperms) to displace the gymnosperms from their preeminent position It is at this stage, that pollen adjacent to the megasporangium, again commence growth. Pollen grains germinate to form a tube that will grow through nuclear tissue and deliver the sperm to the egg. However, up to this point in time, egg is not formed and the megasporocytes have not even undergone meiosis! About a month after pollination, the megaspore mother cells (megasporocytes) undergoes meiosis. It is almost a year later when the two or three archegonia will form towards the micropylar end of the megagametophyte. The pollen tube eventually reaches the archegonium containing the egg cell, and delivers the two recently formed sperm cells. One sperm fertilizes the egg, and the other dies.

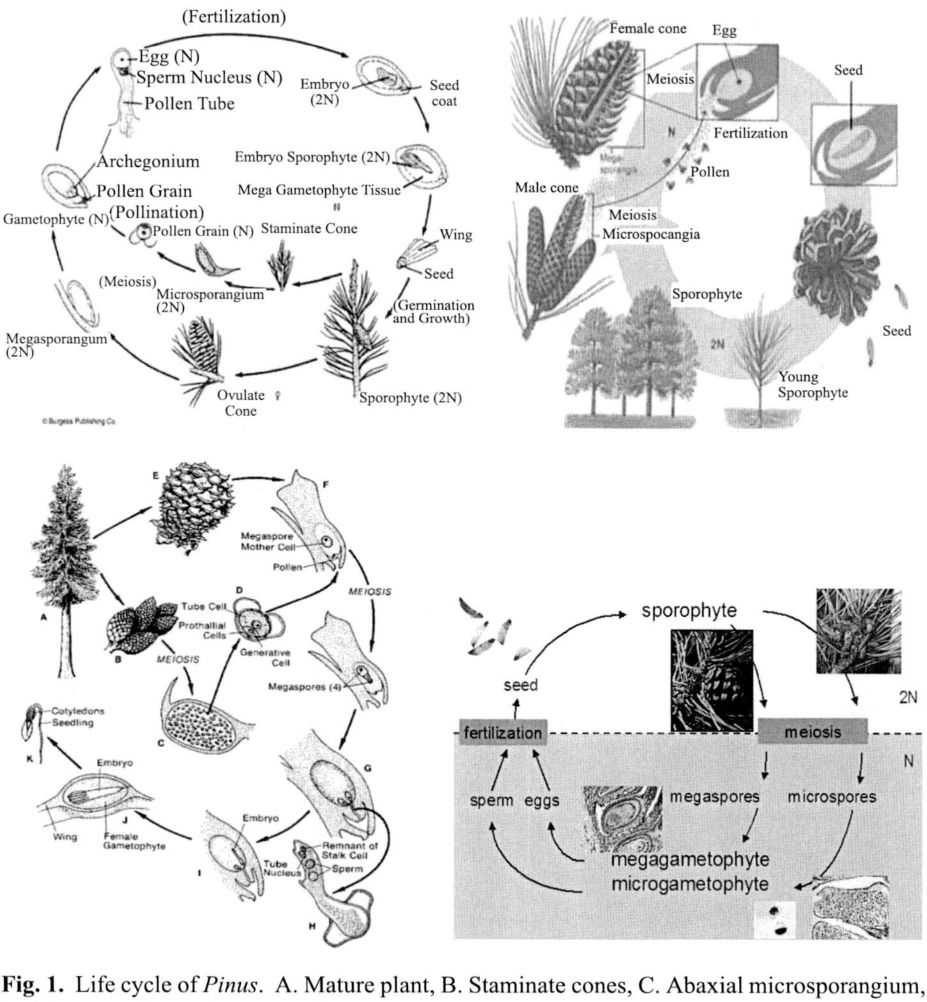

Fig. 1. Life cycle of *Pinus*. A. Mature plant, B. Staminate cones, C. Abaxial microsporangium, D. Mature pollen grain, E. Ovulate cone, F. Pine ovule on the adaxial surface of the ovulate cone scale illustrating pollination, G. Fertilization after the pollen tube enters the archaegonial chamber, H. Detail of the pollen tube with the two sperm, I. Maturing seed with endosperm and embryo, J. Mature seed with developed embryo, K. A germinating seedling (*Source*: Norstog, 1976 and *faculty.clintoncc.suny.edu/faculty/michael.../files/.../seedplants.htm*).

Phylum Cycadophyta - The cycads

Cycades are dioecious and produce seeds on specialized leaves. While male individuals bear microsporophylls organized into microstrobili, the female individuals bear megasporophylls usually organized into megastrobili pollinated by insects and having motile sperm. The pollen finds its way into the micropyle and germinates in the pollen chamber of the ovule. The microgametophyte matures and forms a haustorium, called a pollen tube, that slowly feeds on the megasporangial wall. In the mean time, the megaspore mother cell undergoes meiosis and aborts three of the daughter megaspores. The resulting megaspore begins to grow and develop into a megagametophyte. In the case of *Zamia*, the megagametophyte develops from December to June at which point multiple archegonia reduces to an egg with two neck canal cells. The pollen tube enters the archegonial chamber and multiflagellated sperm, two per pollen grain, and swims to the archegonia. Fertilization occurs in June and the embryonic dicotyledonous plant develops within the maturing seed until November. The seeds are released and germination of the seed occurs after several months of dispersal (Fig. 2).

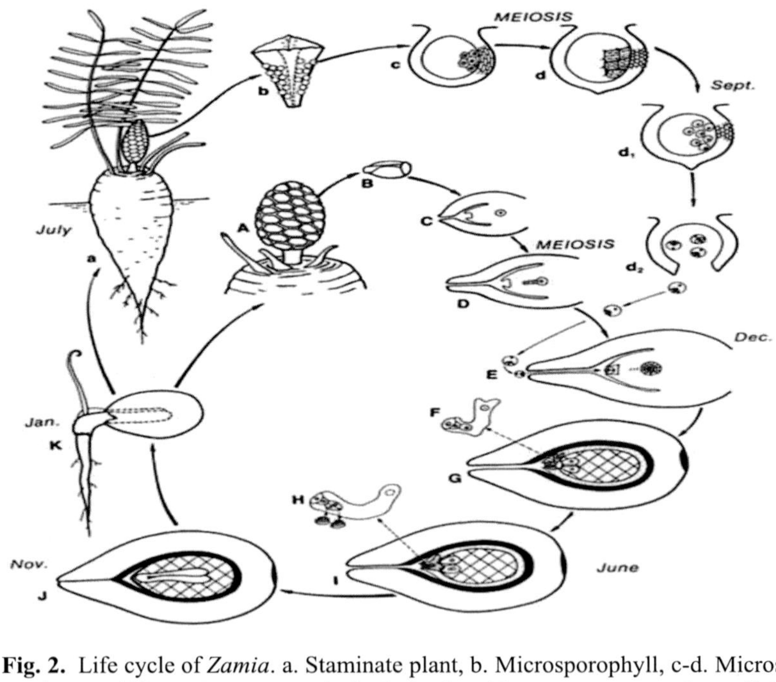

Fig. 2. Life cycle of *Zamia*. a. Staminate plant, b. Microsporophyll, c-d. Microsporangium. A. Ovulate strobilis, B. Megasporophyll, C. Ovule with a megaspore mother cell, D. Linear tetrad of megaspores following meiosis, E. Pollination, F. Pollen tube from microgametophyte, G. Megagametophyte with several archegonia, H. Mature microgametophyte, I. Fertilization, J. Seed with embryo, K. Germinating seed. (*Source:* Norstog, 1976)

Phylum Ginkgophyta - Ginkgo

Ginkgo biloba is dioecious. The ovules and staminate strobili emerge from the spur shoots. The ovules are borne in pairs at the tips of specialized and highly reduced megasporophylls. The other details of the *Ginkgo* life history are similar to that of *Pinus* (Fig. 3).

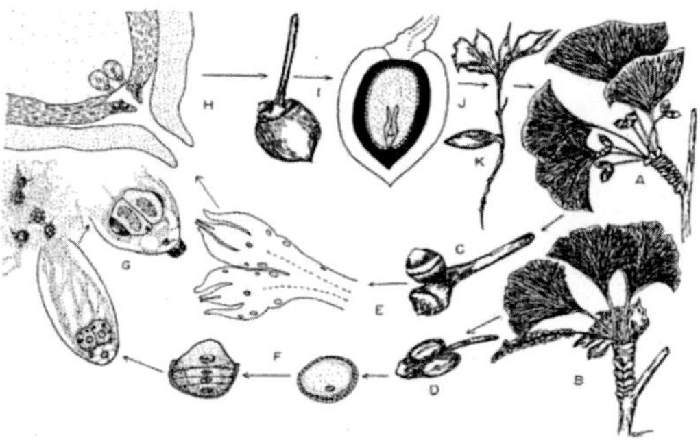

Fig. 3..Life cycle of *Ginkgo biloba*. This species is dioecious: ovulate (A) and staminate (B). two ovules on a

Phylum Gnetophyta - The gnetophytes

The development of pollen in gnetophytes is similar to that of *Pinus*. Pollination is also effected in a way similar to that of Pinus (by exuding a droplet that catches the pollen and pulls them back through the elongate micropyle. The only difference is that the two sperm may participate in the life history differently. Friedman (1990a, 1990b, 1992 and 1994) reported that while one sperm fertilizes an egg, the other fuses with gametophyte tissue, a process called double fertilization (Fig. 4).

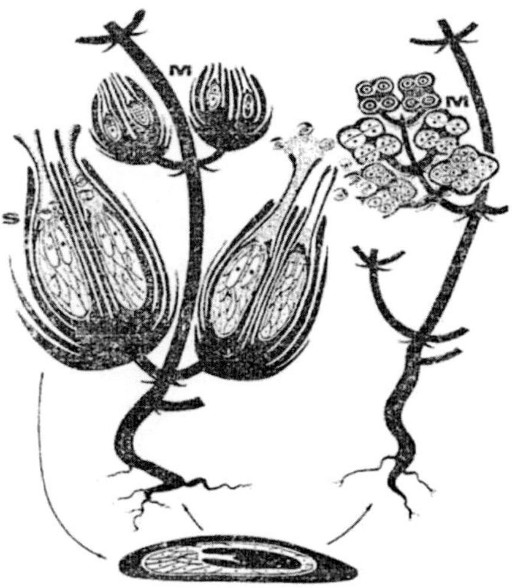

Fig. 4. The life history of *Ephedra*. The axis on the right has a compound microstrobilus, whose microsporangia release pollen. The axis on the left is a compound megastrobilus that illustrates the development of the megagametophyte, each with more than one archegonium. Pollen are caught at the tip of the elongate micropyle and pulled into the pollen chamber where the microgametophyte germinates and grows the pollen tube into the archegonial chamber, where, in *Ephedra* as in the flowering plants, double fertilization occurs. M= meiosis. S= syngamy (*Source:* Cocucci and Hunziker, 1976).

Table 1: Average size of some West Himalayan conifers

Plant species	Female cone (cm)		Shape
	Length	Breadth	
Cedrus deodara	7-13	5-9	barrel-shaped
Pinus wallichiana	16 to 32	3.5 to 7	long and slender
Pinus roxburghii	12–24	5–8	ovoid conic
Pinus gerardiana	10–18	9–11	
Abies spectabilis	14-20	5-7	barrel-shaped
Abies pindrow			barrel-shaped
Picea smithiana	9-16	3-5	broad cylindric-conic

Table 2: Main differences in reproductive cycle of Angiosperms and Gymnosperms

S.No	Angiosperms	Gymnosperms
1	Male and female organs in the same flower (hermaphrodite) or in separate flowers.	Male and female organs always borne separately.
2	Pollen produced in anthers in male or hermaphrodite flowers.	Pollen produced in microsporangia on microsporophylls.
3	Ovules enclosed in pistils or carpels.	Ovules borne open in the megasporophylls.
4	Pollination by wind, water or animals.	Pollination by wind.
5	Pollen deposited on stigma.	Pollen deposited on a pollination droplet at the tip of the intugement.
6	Megasporogenesis (meiosis and formation of egg cell) usually prior to pollination.	Megasporogenesis usually after pollination.
7	Fertilization occurs soon after pollination.	Pollen remains dormant for a longer period of time in pollen chamber or archegonal chamber prior to fertilization.
8	Double fertilization: one sperm cell unites with the egg cell to form zygote, the other fuses with the central cell to form triploid endosperm.	Single fertilization, sperm cell fuses with the egg cell to form zygote.
9	Endosperm made up of triploid tissue of both maternal and paternal genetic origin.	Endosperm made up of haploid maternal tissue.
10	Usually short reproductive cycle.	Usually long reproductive cycle.
11	Ovaries and ovules are small at the time of pollination.	Seed bearing structures and ovules often of near mature size at the time of pollination.
12	Unfertilized ovules usually abort.	Unfertilized ovules remain as empty seeds.

(*Source*: Schmidt, L 2000)

Pollination and fertilization failure

The factors responsible for failure of Pollination and fertilization are:

Shortage of pollen production

In dioecious species it can be caused by accidental removal or less representation of male trees in forests or plantations, which serve as seed production areas or seed orchards (Janzen and Vazquez-Yanes, 1991). Weather conditions and exposure may influence pollen production. For instance dry and exposed conditions are known to favour female flowering and restrict male flowering.

Lack of pollination agents

The fertilization failure may also be caused due to absence of pollination agents or unfavourable environmental conditions during the female receptivity. Wind pollinated species obviously depend on a critical wind velocity and direction in order to efficiently transfer the pollen cloud. Wind velocity may be a limiting factor for long-distance pollination, i.e. between distant trees but is probably insignificant in stands. Further, wind pollination is more likely to be obstructed by moist weather, which may restrict transport of wind-borne pollen (Sedgley and Griffin, 1989). Cold and moist weather may also restrict the activity of animal pollinators, primarily insects. For example, in oil palm plantations (*Hevea brasiliensis*) fruit and seed set is believed to be constrained by shortage of beetle pollinators (Henderson, 1986).

Similarly, heavy rains may also prove to be a limiting factor. For e.g. failure of seed setting in *Gliricidia sepium* has been found to be caused due to heavy rains by preventing pollen transfer during flowering (Gutteridge and Stur 1994). In some exotic species a certain period of adaptation is necessary before effective pollination is achieved by local pollinators. An example is bat pollinated *Calliandra calothyrsus* (Bawa and Krugman 1991). This South American species has faced pollination problems in Africa, and it seems that local bats take some time to recognize this species as a source of food before pollination.

Closed flowers

Cold, moist weather may cause flowers or cones to remain closed at a time when they should be pollinated, and fertilization will consequently fail.

Inbreeding barrier

Most species contain some degree of physiological mechanism in order to minimize inbreeding. Yet inbreeding is a common phenomenon in trees which often causes physiological stresses and self-pollinated flowers or cones are therefore often aborted (Owens, 1995). Inbreeding is obviously a higher risk in isolated trees than in mixed populations.

Cone/ Seed maturity in Gymnosperms

Gymnosperms are characterized by extremely long time period between differentiations of the reproductive organs and seed maturity. Typical examples are many coniferous species like Picea, Tsuga, Larix, and Abies. Cone maturity usually takes about two years time in this genus. In tropical pines, average interval of 23 months has been recorded in Pinus kesiya (Armitage and Burley 1980), 18–21 months in P. oocarpa (Robbins 1983). Some temperate pines (e.g. Pinus contorta), araucarias and podocarps have a reproductive cycle of almost 3 years. A few species like Pinus merkusii complete the reproduction in about 12 months (Owens and Blake 1985). Yellow cypress (Chmaecyparis nootkatensis) fertilization and partial seed development occur in first year, after which the seed ceases development, over winter and matures in second growing season. In such species, pollination occurs in year n, the cones enlarge during the spring and summer of this year, but the actual fertilization of the egg does not take place until late spring of year n+1. (Fig. 5).

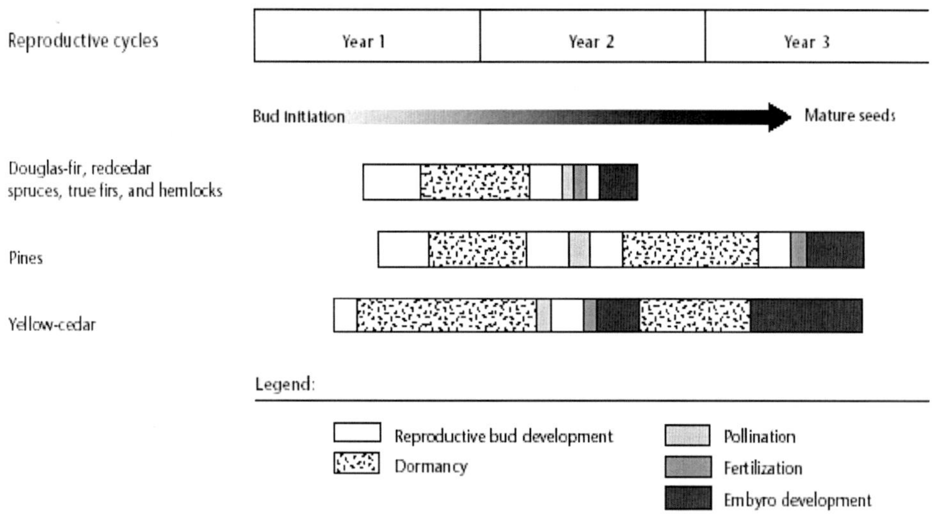

Fig. 5. Maturation cycles of conifer seeds (adapted from Eremko *et al.,* 1989).

Colour of fruits or cones

Colour changes in fruit or cone provide a simple and more reliable criterion for judging seed maturity in some species. The operator, however, must be experienced enough in the characteristics of the species concerned. Fruit colour usually changes from the vegetative green to various shades of yellow, brown or grey and this may be accompanied by hardening of cone scales or of the pericarp of dehiscent or woody fruits.

Abscission and shedding

Abscission of seeds normally occurs between the funiculus and the seeds, i.e. the hilum. In some species like Acacia, the funicle develops into an aril which has a dispersal function, and the abscission zone is consequently formed near the base of the funicle leaving the latter attached to the seed during dispersal. In wind-dispersed pods of some legumes like Albizia, Atrocarpus and some acacias the seeds remain attached to half of the dehiscent pod during dispersal. In Erythrina poeppigiana the seeds remain attached to the entire open pod during wind dispersal (Fig. 6).

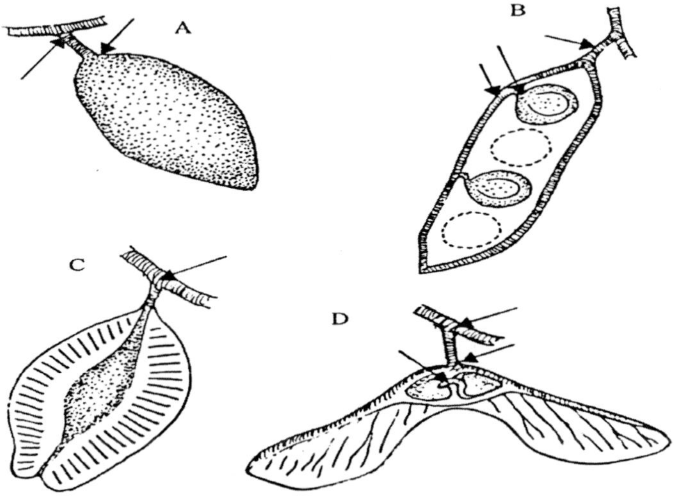

Fig. 6. Examples of location of abscis-sion zones in some fruits. *(Source: Schmidt, L,2000)*

A. Drupe, abscission zones above and below the pedicel (*e.g. Maesopsis eminii).*

B. Dehiscent pod, abscission zones above (occasionally below) pedicel and above or below funicle (*e.g. Acacia sp.*).

C. Samara, abscission zone usually above pedicel (*e.g. Terminalia sp.*).

D. Double samara, abscission zones above or below pedicel and between the two halves (*e.g. Acer sp.*).

Seed dispersal in Angiosperms and Gymnosperms

Unlike animals, plants are limited in their ability to seek out favorable conditions for life and growth. Consequently, plants have evolved many ways to increase their population through their seeds. The unit of dispersal is often called diaspore (Fahn and Werker 1972, Pijl 1982).In order to avoid confusion as to what exactly is being dis-persed, e.g. the fruit, part of the fruit or only the seed. The purpose of dispersal is to colonize new ground. Seed dispersal of a particular species depends on a specific environment in which it lives. Some species are entirely adapted to one mode of dispersal, e.g. species dispersed by animal may even rely on one, or few, species of animals. Others are much less specialized, e.g. some acacias that may be dispersed by wind, water or large herbivores.

Dispersal by wind (enemochory) is assisted when the seeds are very light and small e.g. Eucalyptus. Such species have a large surface/volume ratio and need no additional structures to be carried by wind. In species like Salix, Ceiba, Dyera, seedcoat bears hairy cotton and in Triplochiton, Pterocarpus, Koompassia, Casuarina, Fraxinus pericarp possesses wings to prolong flight. Fruits may also be winged by the enlargement of persistent sepals (most Dipterocarps) or persistent petals (e.g. Gluta, Swintonia) (Krugman *et al.* 1974, Ng 1981) (Fig 7).

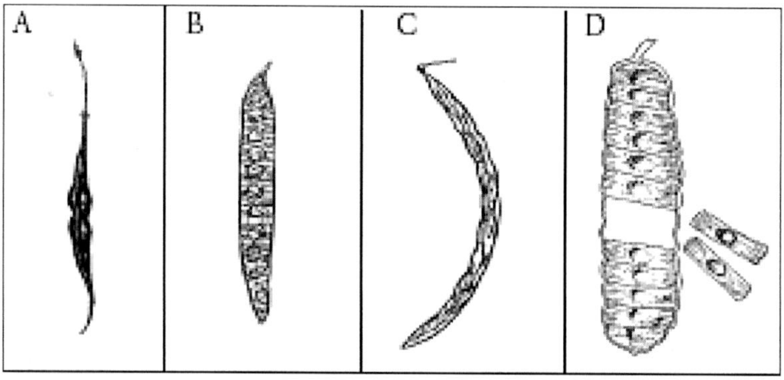

Fig. 7. Dispersal units of some wind-dispersed Leguminosae. *(Source: Schmidt, L,2000)* A. Erythrina poeppigiana, seeds remain attached to the entire open pod during dispersal. B. Albizia gummifera, seeds are attached to one half of the dehiscent pod. C. Acacia seyal, the entire infructescence is often shed and dispersed as a unit. D. Entada abyssinica, the pod consists of segments, which are dispersed separately.

Animal dispersal (zoochory) encompasses a vast number of adaptations and morphological structures. It occurs in all forest types but is most prevalent in closed and stable forests such as rain forests, monsoon forests or savannas. Pijl (1982) distinguishes between types in which the diaspore adheres to fur or plumage of animals and the types in which the diaspore is ingested (eaten) by the animal and the seed (endocarp in drupes) is discharged by the faeces or spat out, and types in which the diaspores are collected by animals as a food. The former type usually has hooks (e.g. Fagus) or sticky substances (e.g. Pisonia, Cordia) to promote adherence. Diaspores, which are dispersed by being eaten include are berries (Antiaris, Citrus), drupes (Maesopsis, Prunus, Azadirachta), pods (some acacias like A.nilotica and A.tortilis, and Prosopis spp.), many multiple fruits (Ficus, Artocarpus and Morus species) and seeds with arils (e.g. many Australian acacias).

General features of ingestive dispersed diaspores are their conspicuousness and a hard tissue (seed-coat or endocarp) to protect them against being digested. Exceptions are found in some very specialized endozoo-chorous diaspores, which are adapted to the ingestion of one or a few species of animals (McKey 1975). An example of the latter is the diaspores of the Dobera glabra, which are ingested and dispersed by hornbills. These diaspores are greenish at maturity (i.e. quite inconspicuous) and have a very thin seed coat, which apparently is not damaged by ingestion. Animal dispersed diaspores are normally quite large; if the seeds are small (e.g. Ficus), they are always congregated in a larger fleshy fruit. Conspicuousness normally develops at a late stage of the maturation period, normally as a visual change of colour or, for diaspores dispersed by nocturnal animals like bats and boars with a strong olfactory sense (Pijl 1982, Fahn and Werker 1972).

Wind and animals are the most important agents of dispersal, but dispersal by water (hydrochory) is common in some riverine species and large and heavy fruits are distributed to some extent by gravity on steep slopes (Krugman *et al.* 1974). Dispersal by water is not common among forest trees although tidal water is the main dispersal agent of mangrove species like Rhizophora and Avicennia. Many riverine species are dispersed by water streams and show adaptation to water dispersal by having air spaces in their fruits (e.g. Acacia nilotica and Sclerocarya bireaa). Since riverine dispersal is essentially downstream, such species always have other accompanying dispersal adaptations.

- The morphological structures (form, size, structure) of fruits and seeds as reflected in their dispersal adaptations have a direct influence on all types of seed handling procedures, particularly harvesting techniques.
- Fruiting season for animal dispersed species is often longer than for wind or water dispersed species, an apparent adaptation of the former to the limited number of dispersal agents (Mckey 1975, Janzen 1978).
- Seeds dispersed by ingestion, e.g. some acacias, usually require a much harsher pre-treatment prior to germination than wind dispersed species from the same environment. The above-mentioned very specialized diaspores adapted to one or a small group of specialized dispersal agents are exceptions.
- Knowledge of dispersal strategies and mechanisms is important for the determination of appropriate harvest time. Firstly, maturation of

dispersal structures has a direct link to the maturation of the seeds, i.e. maturity indices. Secondly, dispersal may limit the time available for seed collection.

References

Armitage, F.B. and Burley, J. (1980): Pinus kesiya Royle ex Gordon (syn. P. khasya Royle; P. insularis Endlicher). Trop. For. Paper No. 9. Comm. For. Inst. Oxford.

Bawa, K.S. and Krugman, S.L. 1991: Reproductive biology and genetics of tropical trees in relation to conservation and management. In: Rain forest regeneration and management (Gomez-Pompa, A., Whitmore, T.C. and Hadley, M., eds.). Man and the Biosphere Series, Vol 6. 119-136. Unesco.

Boland, D.J., Brooker, M.I.H., Turnbull, J.W. and Kleinig, D.A. (1980): Eucalyptus seed. Division of For. Res., CSIRO Canberra.

Chaw S.-M., C. L. Parkinson, Y. Cheng, T. M. Vincent, and J. D. Palmer. 2000. seed plant phylogeny inferred from all three plant genomes: Monophyly of extant gymnosperms and origin of Gnetales from Conifers. Proceedings of the National Academy of Sciences (USA) 97:4086-4086.

Cocucci, A. and A. Hunziker. 1976. Los ciclos biologicos en el Reino Vegetal. Ed. Academia Nacional de Ciencias. Cordoba.Doyle, J. A. 2005. Seed ferns and the origin of angiosperms. Journal of the Torrey Botanical society. 133: 169-209.

Cram, W.H. and Worden, H.A. (1957): Maturity of white spruce cones and seed. For. Sci. 3: 263–269.

Dittmer, H. J. 1964. Phylogeny and Form in the Plant Kingdom. Van Norstrand Company, Inc. New York.

Doyle, J. A. 2006. Seed ferns and the origin of angiosperms. Journal of the Torrey Botanical Society. 133(1): 169-209.

Fahn, A. and Werker, E. 1972. Anatomical mechanisms of seed dispersal. In: Seed Biology. (Kozlowski, T.T., ed.). Vol I. 152-221. Academic Press, New York and London.

Friedman, W. E. 1990a. Double fertilization in Ephedra, a nonflowering seed plant: its bearing on the origin of angiosperms. Science 247:951-954.

Friedman, W. E. 1990b. Sexual reproduction in Ephedra nevadensis (Ephedraceae): further evidence of double fertilization in a nonflowering seed plant. American Journal of Botany. 77:1582-1598.

Friedman, W. E. 1992. Evidence of a pre-angiosperm origin of endosperm: implications for the evolution of flowering plants. Science 225:336-339.

Friedman, W. E. 1994. The evolution of embryogeny in seed plants and the developmenal origin and early history of endosperm. American Journal of Botany. 81:109:153-226.

Gutteridge, R.C. and Stur, W.W. 1994: Seed production for forage tree legumes. In: For-age tree legumes in tropical agriculture (Gutteridge, R.C. and Stur, W.W., eds.).

Henderson, A. 1986. A review of pollination studies in Palmae. Botanical Review 52, 221-259.

Hilton, J. and Bateman, R. M. (2006). Pteridosperms are the backbone of seed-plant phylogeny. Journal of the Torrey Botanicaal Society. 133(1): 119-168.

Janzen, D. 1978. Seeding patterns of tropical trees. In: Tropical trees as living systems (Tomlinson, P.B. and Zimmermann, M.H., eds.). 83-128. U.P. Cambridge.

Janzen, D. and Vazquez-Yanes, C. 1991: Aspects of tropical seed ecology of relevance to management of tropical forested wildland management. In: Rain forest regenera-tion and management (Gomez-Pompa, A., Whitmore, T.C. and Hadley, M., eds.). Man and the Biosphere series, Vol. 6. 137-157. Unesco.

Krugman, S.L., Stein, W.I. and Schmitt, D.M. (1974): Seed Biology. In Seeds of Woody Plants in the United States, Agriculture Handbook No. 450. For. Service. USDA, Washington D.C.

McKey, D. 1975. The ecology of coevolved seed dispersal systems. In: The coevolution of animals and plants (Gilbert, L.E. and Raven, P.H., eds). 159-191. University of Texas Press, Austin and London.

Nagalingum, N. S., C. R. Marshall, T. B. Quental, H. S. Rai, D. P. Little, and S. Matthews. 2011. Recent synchronous radiation of a living fossil. Science. 334(6057): 795-799.

NG, F.S.P. (1981): Vegetative and reproductive phenology of Dipterocarps. Mal. Forester Vol. 44, Nos. 2 & 3.

Owans, J.N. and Blake, M.D. (1985). Forest tree seed production. Can. For. Serv. Petawawa National Forest Institute., Chalk River, Ovt., Info. Rep.Pl-X-53

Pearson, L. C. 1995. The Diversity and Evolution of Plants. CRC Press. New York.

Pijl, L. van der 1982. Principles of dispersal in higher plants. Springer Verlag. Berlin, Heidelberg, New York.

Ran, J-H., H. Gao, X-Q. Wang. 2010. Fast evolution of the retroprocessed mitochondrial rps3 gene in Conifer II and further evidence for the phylogeny of gymnosperms. Molecular Phylogenetics and Evolution. 54: 136-149.

Robbins, A.M.J. (1983): DANIDA Forest Seed Centre, seed leaflet No. 3, Pinus oocarpa Schiede (mimeo).

Schmidt, L. 2000. Guide to handling of tropical and sub-tropical forest seed. Danida Forest Seed Centre, Humlebaek, Denmark

Sedgley, M. and Griffin, A.R. 1989. Sexual reproduction of seed crops. Academic Press.

Singh, H. and Johri, B.M. (1972): Development of gymnosperm seeds. In Seed Biology (Ed. T.T. Kozlowski) Vol. 1 21–75.

Zhong, B., O. Deusch, V. V. Goremykin, D. Penny, P. J. Biggs, R. A. Atherton, S. V. Nikiforova, and P. J. Lockhart. 2011. Systematic error in seed plant phylogenomics. Genome Biology and Evolution. 3: 1340-1348.

Zhong, B., T. Yonezawa, Y. Zhong, and M. Hasegawa. 2010. The position of Gnetales among seed plants: overcoming pitfalls of chloroplast phylogenomics. Molecular Biology and Evolution. 27(12): 2855-2863.

2

Seed Collection and Processing

The collection of cones/fruits and seeds is the first step in the harvest, processing, and storage of seed in which man interacts with nature in determining ultimate seed quality. Successful collection, therefore, depends on understanding seed maturation and dispersal characteristics of each species, knowing local weather trends, and evaluating crop quality. Collection of propagating material is an expensive process and it is therefore also important that areas wherein cones and seeds are to be collected are evaluated to determine whether a sufficiently heavy crop to permit economic collection of seeds is present and whether the seed zone and elevation represented by the candidate area is appropriate for the production of seedlings needed in the reforestation program. Remember that properly collected, processed, and stored seeds may remain viable for a decade, so evaluation of seed needs may be projected well in advance of current harvest schedules through proper planning and organization of seed collection.

Planning seed collection

Planning seed collection involves the determination of crop periodicity, long-term seed requirements, selection of actual collection areas, crop forecasting, crop rating, cone and seed evaluation and pre-collection organization. Seed collector should therefore have some basic knowledge about the following requirements before going for actual planning and organization of the work.

Obtain permission

Laws protected range of native flora. Permits are required for collecting on public land and for some species on private land also. Initial enquiries can be directed to the State national parks service, or the forest service or State herbarium.

Identify species

Correct species identification is vital and several excellent field guides are available. If you are doubtful, forward a botanical specimen (leaves, fruits and flowers or buds pressed between sheets of newspaper or blotting paper) together with a description of the tree's location, size, general appearance and bark to your nearest State herbarium for checking.

Locate suitable collecting sites

Seek advice from local forestry staff, State herbaria or others with local knowledge, or refer to books which show species distribution.

Decide when to collect

Check the literature for guidance on flowering and seeding times and, if possible, visit trees regularly to check on seed ripeness and availability. From early spring to late summer can be especially busy for collectors. Allow for the fact that heat waves and bursts of hot windy weather can accelerate ripening and seed drop in species like wattles. In a 'seed year' the seed quality is better and harvesting is easier.

Assemble the right equipment

It is very important to make sure that the equipment to be used is in a good condition. For small collections you may simply need a few paper bags and some secateurs but detailed planning is required for large collections at remote sites.

Play it safe

Safety precautions will vary with local conditions, tree species and collection methods used. Some safety hints are: work as a team; wear appropriate clothes, safety hat and footwear; and take a first aid kit. Seeds can often be collected safely from the ground or by using a step ladder, but if you plan to climb high trees, take extra care.

Determining crop periodicity

The mechanism ('s) which stimulate perennial plants, such as conifers, to produce flowers are not known. Certainly the process must be more complex than it is with annuals because the latter can convert all of their apical meristems to flowers under a given environment (usually a specified photoperiod) because they do not need to be concerned with reserving some meristems to produce buds for the following year's growth. However, when perennial plants flower they must reserve sufficient meristems in the vegetative state to provide for shoot elongation in the following year. It is difficult, then, to imagine the character of the signal which stimulates part, but not all, of the apical meristems on a given tree to produce reproductive buds. (Table 1).

Table 1: Seed periodicity of some important tree species.

Tree species	Age of first good seed crop (Years)	Age of maximum production (years)	Seed periodicity (Years)
Abies grandis Dougl ex Don	40	45-60	2-3
Abies laciocarpa Hook	20	45-60	2-4
Abies procera	20	40-60	2-4
Abies pindrow	50	150-200	15-20
Euclyptus grandis			2– 3
Dipterocarps			3- 6
E. camaldulensis			2– 3
E. maculate			4 –5
E. saligna			2– 3
Fagus sylvatica			5-10
Larix laricina (Du Roi)	40	50-65	3-6
Larix leptolepis	15-20	40-60	3-4
Larix occidentalis Nutt.	25		1-10
Picea glauca	40		6
Picea abies	30-35	50-60	4-5
Picea mariana	10		4
Picea smithiana	30	150-180	6-10
Picea sitchensis	25-40	40-50	3-5
Pinus flixilis James	20-30		2-4
Pinus monticola Dougl			3-7
Pinus pondsora	12-16		4-6
Pinus sylvestris	15-20	60-100	2 – 3
Pinus kesiya			1– 2
Pinus contorta	15-20		2-4
Pseudotsuga menziesii	20-35	50-60	2-10
Quercus robur			3-5
Tectona grandis			3 – 4
Thuja plicata	20-30	40-60	2-4
Tsuga heterophylla	25-30	40-60	3-4

Source: Seal *et al.*, 1965; Howland and Bowen 1977; Kemp 1973; Keiding 1973; Murthy 1973; Turnbull 1975.

Factors influencing crop periodicity

- Site - Poor sites seem to stimulate early seed production.
- Climate - strong relationships are not clear.
- Insects and Disease - effects most noticeable in light seed years.
- Physiological – not clearly understood.
- Wind, water, animals - most seeds are dispersed close to parent - 40 to 50 meters; advantage = local adaptation, disadvantage = growing in competition with parent

Determining Seed requirement

The first step in the development of and cone and seed collection program is to determine the amount of seeds; by species and provenances, required to meet reforestation needs over a given planning period. It is important to not only to secure adequate supply of seeds but also to plan for collection of future crops to ensure continuous seed supply during poor crop years.

Table 2: Estimation of seed demand

1.	**Species**			**(A)**	**(B)**
2.	Plants per ha				
	(a)	Number planted		1670 (3 × 2 m)	1111 (3 × 3 m)
	(b)	Additional for replacing field casualties			
			- percent	15	35
			- number of plants	250	389
	(c)	Total requirement - plantable plants		1920	1500
	(d)	Additional for nursery losses and culls			
			- percent	20	62.5
			- number of plants	480	2500
	(e)	Total requirement - germinated seedlings		2400	4000
3.	Estimated number of germinated seedlings per kg of seed received			32000	500
4.	Number of kg of seed needed per ha of plantation			0.07 (13.3 ha/kg)	8.0 (0.12 ha/kg)
5.	Annual planting area (ha)			12000	5000
6.	Annual requirement of seed (kg)			900	40000

Identification of areas for seed collection

To identify areas from which seeds need to be collected, the province has been divided into seed planning zones. These zones represent broad climatic regions which may represent biogeo-climatic classification. Within each seed planning zone, transfer rules should describe the maximum movement from the original seed source in which seedlings of a given species be expected to maintain full adaptability. Seed planning zones and transfer rules are used in the annual estimation of seedling requirements. Any difference between requirements and availability indicates where and for which species a shortage may occur during planning period.

Crop forecasting and rating

The next step in planning potential collections is to forecast the probability of successful crop development in specific collection areas. Early crop forecasting is generally accomplished through bud sampling. This involves collecting a branch from several well-distributed trees in each stand being surveyed. Trees used in bud sampling should be dominant or co-dominant in the stand with well developed crowns and ideally should be between 45 and 80 years of age. Older trees or those whose branches have been distorted from previous crops and/or collections are not suitable. By late winter/early spring of the crop year, buds may be identified by recognizeable external characteristics or by internal features that are visible after the buds have been sectioned with a razor blade or scalpel. All female buds on the branch from the tip to three internodes back are counted and recorded for each tree.

The exact quantitative relationship between female bud counts and size of the crop remains obscure for most species. The word potential is stressed, since the many impedimences to cone and seed development may at any stage cause the reproductive structures to abort or may destroy the maturing seeds. In other words, bud sampling can result in conclusion about whether a crop might develop. A collectable crop is not ensured until shortly before collection. When sectioned, the tissues of reproductive buds will be seed to fill the bud cavity more than they do in vegetative buds. Female buds tend to be larger, more pointed and broader at the base than male buds. When sectioned or exposed by removal of bud scales, female buds have a distinct cone like structure whereas male buds have a raspberry like appearence. Male buds often occur in clusters while female buds are frequently single.

Cone crop rating is highly subjective and largely dependent on the surveyer's experience. Of particular importance is the surveyer's understanding of the cone production characteristics of the species being assessed. In developing judgements about few and many cones, attention should be confined only to the cone-bearing portion of the crown. In true firs cone production is limited to the top four or five whorls, whereas in cedars cones occur throughout the crown. Medium and heavy crops are collectable; however, in the case of severe seed shortages, crops rated as "4" may also be collected to meet intermediate seed needs.

Errors in rating cone crops commonly arise when old cones are included as part of current crop and when evaluation is restricted to roadside trees which because of their increased exposure to sunshine often bear more cones than do those within the stand. Unless the crop is only to be harvested from roadside trees, both crops result in over estimation of crop size. Each stand must have sufficient number of cone bearing trees to meet collection quotas and to be cost effective. Based on results obtained from cone crop ratings, potential collection areas are selected. These areas will continue to be reassessed throughout the maturation period to determine seed quantity, maturity and overall condition.

Monitoring the seed crop

The sequence and length of different components of the reproductive cycle must be understood when planning and executing seed production studies because different components are not the same in each species. For example, you need to know the length of the entire reproductive cycle of each species involved in the study, since this will determine when monitoring should begin. You must also know the timing of other critical events, such as pollination, fertilization, and periods of bud dormancy, to ensure you are at the right place at the right time. For red cedar, spruces, true firs, and hemlocks, the development and maturation cycle takes about 16 months. In pines, complete development takes 26 months because fertilization is delayed for 1 year after pollination. In yellow-cedar, pollination and fertilization take place in the same growing season, but the total cycle usually lasts about 28 months. In hardwoods like maple, alder, birch, Garry oak and willows it is necessary to identify male and female clones before monitoring since they bear male and female flowers on different trees. Besides, as the pollination, fertilization and seed maturation occur within the same year (El-Kassaby *et al.* 1991), the seed crop should be monitored over a period from its development to maturation.

Seed yields in conifers

On an average, there are two seeds in a cone scale and therefore the theoretical yield from a given cone is 2 x the number of cone scales. However, the average maximum yield of seed from a cone is no more than 65 to 70% of this theoretical number because the cone scales at the base and tip of the cone may not bear viable seed because either these scales do not develop the mechanism necessary to assure fertilization or because they do not develop normal ovules and mega-gametophyte tissue. The significance of this behavior to cone collection is that normally the center portion of the cone will open its scales first, releasing the great majority of the sound seed. If cones, which are partially opened, are collected, therefore, the yield of viable seed will be greatly reduced over that which could have been harvested if the cones were collected while still fully closed. Cones that are difficult to cut longitudinally e.g. yellow cedar,, lodgepole pine etc are cut transverselly at the center and the seeds on one cut face are counted. Hand lens is used during evaluation particularly for small seeded species. An alternative more logistic method for evaluating difficult to cut cones involves extracting and cutting individual seeds to determine whether they are filled. The cones are first dipped in water for about one minute or until the sound of cracking resin bonds stops and then drying the cones in an oven at 60° C for about 8 hours.

Studies have shown that for many pine species the maximum cone potential is 85 percent (Bramlett, 1974). This potential then provides us with three measures of accomplishment: actual production from extraction, actual production of cones and potential production. For example, assume that a cone produces 35 seeds after drying and shaking, retained 15 seeds and had enough scales to produce 120 seeds. Using these figures the extraction efficiency would be 70 percent [35 ÷ (15+35) × 100]. Now we have seen that 50 seeds (15 +35) were produced in cones capable of producing 120 seeds. This is the production efficiency 42 percent [50 ÷ 120 × 100]. Thus if extraction is done with care, we could be able to double the seed production from the same number of cones. Van Haverbeke (1976) found that reprocessing of Scotch pine cones by soaking them in water for 30 minutes at 85°F and allowing them to air-dry before reheating could increase the seed yields by one-third.

Table 3: Seed production characteristics of some conifers.

Species	**Cone length (cm)**	**Average viable Seeds (per ht.l of cones)**	**Position of cones in crown**	**Ease of cone Detachment**
Abis grandis	5-12	50776	Top ¼	Difficult
Abies laciocarpa	6-12	40582	Top ¼	Difficult
Abies pindrow				
Cedrus deodara				
Picea glauca	3 - 6	347163	Top ½	Moderate
Picea mariana	2.5	108000	Top ¼	Difficult
Picea sitchensis	5 - 10	194270	Top ½	Moderate
Picea smithiana				
Pinus flixilis James	7 - 20	6454	Throughout	Moderate
Pinus monticola Dougl	10 - 25	7687	Top ¼	Moderate

Pinus pondsora	7 - 9	31522	Throughout	Difficult
Pinus contorta	3 - 6	70546	Throughout	Difficult
Pinus wallichiana				
Pinus roxburghii				
Pseudotsuga menziesii	5 - 10	49577	Top ½	Easy
Thuja plicata	1 -2	897837	Throughout	Easy
Tsuga heterophylla	2 - 3	36698	Throughout	Easy

Table 4: Rating of pine seed crops by number of filled seeds per hectare (Alexander *et al.*, 1982)

Filled seeds (per ha)	Seed crop rating
< 25,000	Failure
25,000 – 1,25,000	Poor
1,25,000 – 2,50,000	Fair
2,50,000 – 6,25,000	Good
6,25,000 – 12,50,000	Heavy
> 12,50,000	Bumper

Note that there may be some discrepancy between the cone crop rating and the number of seeds collected in seed traps. Such discrepancies can occur in areas where there is heavy predation of cones by squirrels. Thus, generally it is best to count when cones have attained maximum physical dimensions, and before squirrels begin to harvest.

Cone and seed analysis is based on calculating four critical ratios (efficiencies), which are used to identify the sources (stages) in which major losses occur (Bramlett *et al.*, 1977).

$$\text{Cone efficiency} = \frac{\text{Number of cones harvested}}{\text{Number of conelets counted}}$$

$$\text{Seed efficiency} = \frac{\text{Number of filled seeds}}{\text{Number of fertile sites}}$$

$$\text{Extraction efficiency} = \frac{\text{Number of extracted seeds per cone}}{\text{Number of total filled seeds per cone}}$$

$$\text{Germination efficiency} = \frac{\text{Number of germinated seeds}}{\text{Number of total filled seeds}}$$

The analysis requires the determination of:

- Potential number of seeds per cone.
- Total number of seeds per cone.
- Number of extracted seeds per cone.

- Number of filled seeds per cone.
- Number of empty and insect damaged seeds per cone.

Pre-collection organization

Whereas planning collection is decision oriented and concerns whether, where and when to collect, pre-collection organization is action oriented and involves activities such as preparing collection areas, accumulating and readying equipment, arranging for pickers and transportation and setting up interm cone storage facilities. When two or more areas are scheduled for collection priorities must be assigned according to seed needs anticipated, anticipated maturation date, species evaluation, location and available labour.

The first step in organizing any cone collection is to determine the most efficient and cost effective method of collecting the crop. The choice of collection method will depend on species, location and funding. Once the collection method has been decided some specific issues must be addressed. For example, if the choice is felling, related matters such as utilization of timber, sale arrangements, permits and other logging details must be considered. Another major concern is proximity to landings, roads or skid trials. The area into which the crowns fall should be relatively clear of brush or slash to facilitate access and cone gathering. Trees to be felled or climbed for cone collection should be marked. The windfalls should also be removed to facilitate access. If collection is to be accomplished by climbing, only trees that permit safe climbing and efficient cone gathering should be selected. If the choice is aerial collection, sufficient space for safe landing and fueling must be available. Landing and picking areas must be positioned so that there is no hazard to pickers.

Crop size, crop density, anticipated picker productivity, supervision required and the collection are major activities of pre-collection organization. Picker productivity depends on many factors such as the size of all cones being collected, efforts required to detach cones from the branch, number of collectable cones, weather and picker motivation. All necessary equipment like collection tools, logging tools, sacks, tags, spray paint, collection report forms first aid kit should be organized before the start of any collection. The supervisor must also ensure that interm cone storage facilities are available within a reasonable distance of the collection site. These interm storage facilities must have a roof and good ventilation.

The quantity and quality of seeds collected and the efficiency of the collection operation will depend not only on the degree of pre collection organization but also on the knowledge and competence of the collection supervisor. Therefore, these persons should get a periodic tranning to update their knowledge not only regarding the latest techniques of collection but also requirements of various species to collect their quality seed.

Determining best dates for seed collection

Seed yields and viability increase with cone and fruit maturity; however, if all collections were delayed until complete maturity, a lot of seed would be lost because of natural seed dispersal. Therefore, cones are usually collected as soon as maturity guides indicate they are ready (Stein et al 1974, McLemore, 1959).

Collection of immature seeds

It is general practice to collect seeds when they are mature, because they have a higher germinative energy and a greater longevity in storage than immature seeds. An alternative method is to collect fruits prior to ripening and to store them in relatively cool, well-ventilated conditions which permit after-ripening of the seeds within the fruit. It has shown promise on a research scale in a number of species. Artificial ripening of Pinus radiata cones, which normally require 30 months from the time of the appearance of the strobilus until cone maturity has been shown to reduce this time by 15 weeks and thus save a year in progeny testing. It should be remembered, however, that artificial ripening will be effective only if the cones are collected no more than 20 days before the anticipated time of seed maturity.

Seed documentation

High physiological and genetic seed quality is tightly linked to a good record and documentation system. From a genetic point of view, seeds without information on its origin, history and potential performance pose a risk and may be almost worthless. Seed records have different purposes for the different people involved, and the documentation system and contents including the level of detail vary accordingly. For example:

1. Seed documentation may be used as a planning tool for future seed procurement. Records on seed collection from various seed sources may provide useful information on productivity, seasonality and periodicity in seeding pattern, thereby saving time on initial surveys prior to collection. Success or failure of achieving good seed quality may often be ascribed to particular handling procedures. Far too much re-invention and re-exploration is made because previous mistakes were not recorded. Poulsen and Thomsen (1999) have proposed a thorough seed procurement record and documentation system with the major

purpose of improving procurement methods by analysing documented practices. The system covers all handling aspects from maturity criteria, collection and processing to testing and storage.

2. Internal database: In small units such as local forest departments, where seed collection, nursery operation and planting are under the same head, documentation may seem redundant. However, human memory has limitations, staff members move or resign, and the life time of trees, which can be important when tracing seed sources, tends to be longer than service in the forest sector.
3. Information and quality documentation for end user (customer): Documentation is a link between supplier and end user. It contains information on both seed source (origin) and test results. Good seed documentation becomes particularly important when seeds are dispatched to end users who are not in direct contact with those who collected and handled the seed. This is particularly so in international transfer of seed. Seed source details, genetic base and physiological quality are factors of major importance for the seed buyer.
4. Requirement from official authorities: Type and details of required seed documentation vary from one country to another and usually depend on quantity, type of disposal, and species. Small non-commercial seed lots distributed within the country e.g. in connection with research are rarely subject to any official requirement of documentation. Commercial seed lots are usually subject to the same type of accounting as any other commercial product. Seed transferred over international borders may be subject to particular regulations and documentation requirements such as:
   a. Customs regulations: Commercial seed lots may be subject to general or specific import regulations e.g. on paying tax and duty, an official invoices are required.
   b. The importing country may require that imported 'living plant material' is free of pest and diseases. Where an official accredited laboratory carries out the examination and/or treatment, the seed lot is issued with an official 'Phytosanitary Certificate'.
   c. Export of forest seed has so far rarely been subject to regulations by the exporting countries. However, with the increasing concern of national right to genetic resources, export regulations are likely to become more common in the future, at least for some species and in some countries. For this special documentation which may need to accompany seeds in transit, especially if movement is between

countries, includes collecting licenses, seed movement orders, export and import permits, phytosanitary certificates and certificates of origin or of genetic value under national or international schemes of seed certification.

5. In special circumstances, for example if seeds are to be sold or displayed, a colour photograph of the parent tree is helpful. Similarly, while dealing with species of uncertain identity, collect herbarium specimens. Keep one as your record and send a duplicate to a herbarium for identification.
6. In a seed store, a seed record card system is a useful method of stock control. On one side of the card summarise the collection data and on the other write details about the distribution of any part of the lot, together with a running total of the amount of seed remaining in stock. As an additional insurance against accidental loss of the exterior label, identical labels should be placed both inside and outside the container.
7. When one seed lot is divided between several containers for dispatch, each label should state also the number of containers involved (e.g. 1 of 4).
8. Additional information for research: The main purpose for documentation of provenance collections or single tree collections for progeny trials is to provide information on conditions of the seed which will assist in interpretation of research results or planning the collection (Kemp 1975a)

Seed suppliers usually design their own forms and documentation system. It should be emphasised that both too much and too little information may be a nuisance. It is important that all relevant information on a seed lot is available, but not all information need to be provided to any user. For example, a label adhering to a submitted seed sample need only contain basic information on species, provenance, quantity etc., while additional information is submitted on a separate form. It is therefore important that each seed lot be allocated a unique seed identity number, which will appear on any information form of the same seed lot, and from which specific seed lot information can be retrieved.

Seed documentation is usually filled in on predesigned forms during collection, processing or testing. Reliability of documentation is always a matter of confidence. If a seed collector states that they have collected seeds from 20 widely spaced, good phenotype trees in a superior stand, there is rarely a way to check whether it is true. Unfortunately, much seed is traded above its real quality on that account. A good documentation system is a way to avoid lapse, failures or direct dishonesty in seed procurement, and in turn achieve confidence from customers. The signature by the officer in charge of individual operations should be a guarantee of both appropriate methodology applied (e.g. in testing) and reliability of data.

Codes and accession number system

Codes and reference numbers should be unique, meaning that two species, two seed sources or two seed lots do not have the same code or number. Species may be referred to by three or four first letters of genus and species name, all in capital letters. Three is usually sufficient both to be unique and to recognise the species name from the code, but it becomes easier with four. However, even four is not a safe identification code. For example EUCAMICR may mean both Eucalyptus microtheca and E. microcorys. If one happens to have both these species in supply, they must be distinguished by other means. In fact there are very few examples where 4+4 letters can cause confusion.

Seed-source reference number may consist of numbers, letters or a combination. Letters may refer to species, location, type of seed-source etc. Letters referring to species may cause confusion in case several species are collected from the same seed source. As an example of a seed source reference system, the National Tree Seed Programme (NTSP) in Tanzania uses a system consisting of three components (Rasmussen, 1992):

- Two capital letters, referring to one of the three regional seed centres (RC) responsible for the seed source.
- A three digit serial number referring to seed source identity within the particular RC.
- One capital letter referring to type of seed source e.g. Z (= seed collection zone), I (= identified stand), S (= selected stand), A (= seed production area), P (= provenance seed stand), and O (= seed orchard).

Seeds delivered at the central processing station (forest office, seed centre etc.) may already have been given a provisional or temporary seed lot number for identification in the field. At the beginning of the handling procedure the seed lot is given a new number according to a predecided system, which may differ from place to place. As with seed source the identification or accession number may contain letters, figures or both, which may be related to species, seed source, year of collection etc (Lauridsen, 1994).

Australian Tree Seed Centre uses a continuous 5 digit number for each species (ATSC, 1995). Danida Forest Seed Centre uses a system where seed lots are numbered in sequence as they enter the seed bank, the year of accession being indicated. For e.g a seed lot with identity number 5320/92 means a bulked seed lot number 5320 received in 1992 (Lauridsen 1994). At the NTSP in Tanzania the seed-lot accession number consists of three components:

1. The seed source number (according to the system described above),
2. A two digit number indicating year of collection,
3. A capital letter indicating number of collection in the particular seed source.

Seed-lot accession number MO149S/91B thus refers to the second seed collection (indicated by B) in 1991 (indicated by /91) from above mentioned Morogoro seed source number 149, which is a selected stand (Rasmussen, 1992).

The above examples show that the options are vast and the individual seed supplier must decide on a system, which is appropriate under the particular operation conditions. The most important is that identity or reference numbers are unique, so that two seed sources or seed lots will not have the same number. Once the seed lot number has been allocated, it should be entered on all seed forms and labels subsequently used for that seed lot. Codes and reference numbers for seed suppliers and customers may include letters for country code, region, project etc.

Seed documentation systems

Complete seed documentation systems consist of a variable number of standard forms, which are filled in during seed handling. Examples of seed documentation systems are given by Rasmussen (1992), Lauridsen (1994), and ATSC (1995). Willan (1985) gives examples of forms used by forest seed centres and suppliers all over the world. The predesigned forms are essential for recording data in the field or laboratory. Information and records filled in forms is used for both statistical calculation and other data management (Table 8).

Table 6. Overview of seed record and documentation forms.

Seed source records	Seed source information form (A14.1A) List of seed sources (A14.1B) Country map of seed sources (A14.1C)
Collection and seed handling records	Collection and handling records (A14.1D) Seed procurement accounting form (A14.1E)
Seed testing records	Seed sampling form (A14.1F) Seed test forms (A14.1G1+2)
Seed stock and dispatch records	Seed stock and dispatch form (14.1H)
Customer information	Seed lot summary data sheet (A14.1I) Labels for containers (A14.1J)

Seed source records

Seed source records provide information on the origin of the seed, i.e. from where the seeds were collected & including the ecological conditions of the site and type of seed source. Ecological information such as altitude, rainfall, temperature, and soil type, is essential for matching the right seed source with the particular planting environment. Also seed zone and provenance contain information about site conditions. Seed zones are the largest units in seed collection. The classification of seed zones is based on climatic factors (temperature, precipitation), physiographic structure (topography, geology, soils) and geographical elements (vegetation). Seed zones serve as a broad guideline for transfer-ring seeds for national plantation programmes (Barner and Willan 1985). The provenance name refers more specifically to where the species grows. A seed zone (sometimes called region of provenance) may thus contain several identified provenances. A provenance name normally refers to a relatively well identifiable place on a map, e.g. a lake, hill or nearest larger town. The provenance concept implies that there is a reasonable uniformity and exchange of genetic material within the population that makes up a provenance. Hence, provenance contains ecological and genetic uniformity information

The ecological information of provenances may be a more specific guideline on provenance choice for particular planting sites than seed zone. For example, if one were to plant Pinus caribaea at a lowland moist site, it would probably be advisable to purchase seed from a lowland moist provenance. The provenance name refers to where the species grows, no matter whether it is a natural forest or it was introduced. However, for exotic species the origin should, if possible be indicated.

The type of stand gives information on the genetic history and sometimes quality of the seed source. Neither natural stands nor most plantations have been subject to selection for quality. A natural stand often has a wider genetic base than a plantation unless the natural stand is a small isolated group of trees, e.g. a small relict of a previous large stand. Both natural stands and plantations can be upgraded to selected or certified seed sources or seed stands. The latter involves some selection since inferior individuals must be eliminated to upgrade the average genetic quality. Where a seed source has been established based on genetic results from an improvement programme, the seed source is referred to as a seed orchard. Both generation (1st, 2nd etc.) and mode of establishment (clonal or seedling) are indicated in the seed source record.

Much information on seed-source forms has only relevance to the seed collector or supplier. That pertains to e.g. information on owner-ship, accessibility, size, age and productivity of the stand. Also details on flowering and fruiting periods, potential local labour availability and other pure collection details are of little interest for the seed customer, while being highly relevant for the seed supplier. Only information that refers directly or indirectly to seed quality is transferred to the form submitted to the customer.

Collection and seed handling records

For each individual seed lot, procedures and conditions during seed collection and processing are recorded. As the seed-source reference number appears in the form, collection and handling records can be linked to the particular seed source where the seed was collected. The collection form contains two measures on genetic quality viz. genetic base and selection of seed trees. Genetic base is indicated by the number of and distance between parent trees of the seed lot. This information is important if the plants to be raised may be considered as seed source some time in the future. Information on phenotypic selection of seed trees applies in particular to natural stands and plantations, since selection is already implicit where seeds are collected from seed stands or seed orchards. Phenotypic selection of seed trees is usually done during collection

Information on field handling, transport and possible field processing are particularly important for the further processing at the central processing station. It is envisaged that the first part of the seed handling and processing form is filled in and signed by the person responsible for the collection, before the seed lot form is handed over to the processing station. Many details on collection and handling appearing on the form have relevance only to those involved in seed collection and processing. The information may be used by the seed supplier as a guideline during the succeeding processing of the particular seed lot, and to improve procedures for future seed lots. Seed handling records are especially pertinent where different people are involved in different processes. For example, if field collection records tell that a seed lot was collected during moist weather, the processing officer may give priority to rapid processing of this seed lot. It is therefore an advantage that the seed collection and handling form follows the seed lot during seed handling and is filled in gradually during handling (Poulsen and Thomsen 1999). Expenses of seed collection and processing also need to be recorded on a prescribed form. The accounting system helps to estimate the actual procurement expenses, which form a major component during calculation of seed price. This information may also be used to identify areas where gains in efficiency can be made. It is also useful during planning when demand is matched to potential sites for collection.

Seed testing records

Samples for seed testing are frequently drawn from the bulk seed lot and submitted to the seed-testing laboratory. A seed sampling form should accompany the samples. The form is a documentation that sampling was undertaken according to the rules of representativeness. Seed testing documentation contains results of standard seed testing procedures such as seed weight, moisture content, purity and viability/germination plus sometimes special test. The results are summarised in a seed testing section of the seed lot summary data form. If other viability test than germination is carried out (cutting, X-ray, TTZ etc.), the form should state which type of test has been carried out. Since viability declines with time, the date of testing is important. Regular viability tests are pertinent for long-time storage, and for seed with short viability. Obviously the latest record should be the one submitted to customers.

Testing for seed-borne pests and pathogens may be carried out in connection with general seed testing or by special laboratories. The latter is often a requirement during international transfer, where the phytosanitary condition must be documented on a Phytosanitary Certificate. A phytosanitary certificate always states that the seed is found free of special pathogens, since otherwise it would not be issued. Often it is issued only after treatment of the seed. The document will then state which type of pesticide has been used. This should also always be indicated on more informal seed documentation forms.

Seed stock and dispatch records

These records are essential for management of seed stores, sales or other modes of disposal. In addition the seed-stock records contain the basic information to be used in seed catalogues. The seed stock and dispatch record contains a list of species, provenance, seed lot number, date of collection etc. Seed stock currently changes as new seed lots are collected and enter into the stock, and seed lots are dispatched for sale or local nursery sowing. It is essential that both outgoing and incoming seed lots be consciously registered to keep trace of the seed stock. Where seed of different age is available in the stock, the 'first-in - first-out' principle is adopted. Data of incoming and outgoing stock are essential also for planning future seed collection. Computer databases are particularly useful for stock and dispatch records. Even where the documentation system is mainly manual, tables formed in word processing programmes may be useful for record keeping since new lines can be added as new seed lots appear or parts of seed lots are dispatched.

Customer information

Labels are attached to the seed sample submitted to the customer. The label contains only basic information such as species, seed lot number, quantity etc. Copies of seed handling and testing forms may accompany submitted seed lots, or information may be compiled into a separate summary data form. In addition to the essential seed lot information, the summary form contains brief recommendations on handling from receipt to sowing.

Updating and maintenance of data

Data management consists of collecting, storing and distribution of data. As any new seed lot involves several forms and registers, one would soon end up with piles of paper, if it were all kept in files. Much information may be relevant only to few people and for short time. Both ledger systems and computer databases tend to accumulate vast numbers of outdated data, and a system of erasing irrelevant data soon becomes an important task in data management. Seed testing records would, for instance, normally be of no use once the seed has been sown. Of utmost importance is that the seed origin of any plantation can be traced back to its seed source. If a seed lot happens to give rise to an exceptionally good (or bad!) performance, it is important that the customer (and supplier) is able to trace the source from where the seeds were collected.

Generally, seed-source information is kept as long as the (potential) seed source is there, whether seed is still collected from there or not. However, current information is obviously only updated in those seed sources regularly used. The seed collector must be aware of this since e.g. changed ownership or administration may necessitate new arrangements on collection. If appropriate measures were taken during collection to assure the genetic quality (number, spacing and performance of mother trees), and the seed supplier is likely to keep seed source records, then information on seed source may be redundant for the tree planter. However, in practice such information tends to get lost for various reasons during the lifetime of a forest plantation. Therefore it is advisable that the tree planter keeps essential seed-source information that will enable him/her to trace the seed source.

For the seed supplier, information on a particular seed lot becomes irrelevant once the last seed has been dispatched. In some computer database systems a seedlot will automatically be deleted if its final value is nil. However, the seed supplier should keep records on dispatched seed lots, both as a service to the customer in case some records are lost, and in their own interest since it will help to identify particularly valuable (or poor!) seed sources and provenances.

Data management systems

Data relating to seed sources, seed lots, sales etc. can be handled entirely manually by filling in, filing, copying and submitting forms. More extensive use of personal computers and development of their storage and operation capacity, plus development of user friendly database programmes are nowadays replacing much of the laborious copying work and manual filing system. Databases can be used for statistical analysis and searching, and data storage requires much less space than manual systems. Establishment of computer networks allows quick and efficient entry and reading of data from linked computer terminals. It is therefore especially suitable for handling large numbers of seed lots. Computer systems do not, however, entirely replace manual systems, since forms must often be filled in the field or in the laboratory without access to terminals. An entirely electronic data management system is sensitive to power cuts and computer breakdown and a combination of manual and electronic systems are often preferred.

Most manual data management systems use a set of standard formula. Permanent records such as seed source or plantation data were previously almost exclusively filed in ledgers, a system that is still much used. The ledger system is robust and simple but quite time consuming. The viscard system is a loose-leaf filing system using hard index cards arranged according to a predecided system e.g. species or seed lots. The cards are filed in boxes, arranged so that one or two data lines containing key information is visible without taking out the whole card. Because the cards are relatively small (and expensive), the viscard system is used mainly for particular information like address catalogues, seed-stock register, seed-testing register or the like (Lauridsen 1994). Loose-leaf systems are more flexible than the ledger system and more practical for filing. Original or photocopy of standard forms is normally filed in ring binders according to different systems e.g. species, seed lot, customer, supplier or other system.

Documentation may be filed in standard forms in ordinary word processing systems, but with much data, the system becomes awkward. Simple databases may be set up in DOS based programmes like Dbase and Paradox. Newer data bases based on Window systems, e.g. Access, allow statistical analysis and combination of data from different registers. A complete seed documentation database system has been established for an Indonesian tree seed project (Purmono 1996).

A database consists of a number of registers, each containing one or more key fields plus a number of data fields. Key fields are used for searching information and combing information from different registers. Examples of key fields are species codes, seed source accession code, seed lot accession code, supplier code etc. The same key fields may appear in different registers. Data fields contain specific information related to each register. For example, a seed source register contains data fields of provenance name, locality, ownership etc. Data fields are unique for each register.

Interim seed storage

During the period immediately after collection from the tree seeds are susceptible to damage. Fluctuations of climate cannot be predicted or prevented and transport may involve persons who do not have the same personal interest in the welfare of the seeds as the collector, processor or user. Careful advance planning is therefore essential in order to provide the closest possible control over the identity and health of the seed at all stages. If fruits cannot be transported at once to the seed-processing depot, temporary field storage must be arranged, in sheds or under some kind of shelter. Shelter is needed against rain and, for some species, against too high insulation. Sheds should be open-sided or otherwise well ventilated and sacks well spaced on racks or hung from hooks to allow free air circulation. Hanging from hooks has the added advantage of giving protection against rodents. If storage is in the open, overhead shelter may be provided by canvas tarpaulins or polyethylene sheeting. If the collecting season coincides with a period of reliably dry but not too hot weather, no overhead shelter is necessary. Sacks should never be piled on top of each other in large heaps.

Special measures may be needed to prevent damage from pests and diseases. The use of insecticidal or fungicidal dusts may be advisable in some circumstances, if there is a high risk of severe damage, but great care is needed in treating fresh and relatively moist seed, to avoid damage from the chemicals themselves (Kemp 1975). Maintaining fruit hygiene, particularly through good ventilation, is usually preferable to reliance on chemicals. Storage of sacks off the ground will itself give some protection against rodents. The incidence of pests and diseases is often worst on the forest floor and prompt collection of fallen fruits can do much to minimize subsequent losses.

Table 7: Cone and seed collection standards:

Crop characteristics	Standard
Cone crop rating	5 or more
Filled seed content	Minimum average number acceptable
Maturity	
Embryo	Present and filling at least 90% of the embryonic cavity
	Creamy yellow to pale green
	Cotyledons visible with 10x hand lens
Storage tissue	White
	Not translucent
	Nut like in texture
	Little or no shrinkage after drying
Seed wing	Tan to golden brown
	Brittle after dry ing
	Easily detached from cone scale
Cones	Slight flexing of scale margins
	Golden to medium brown
	Abies may be purplish or greenish grey
Cleanliness	Less than 5% debris and unacceptable cones in collections of all species except Sw, Hw and Cy
	Less than 10% debris in collections of Sw, Hw and Cy
	Less than 25% class III and IV of PL cones
Sacks	Must be made of a material woven in a manner which allows good air circulation and moisture exchange
	Clean, dry and undamaged
	Must contain no more than 0.4 hl of cones
	Must be securely tied near top
	Must display seed lot number clearly and have attached a completed shipping tag with duplicate copy inside
Temporary Storage	Sacked cones must be shaded, dry and well ventilated
	Sacks must be racked lying flat
	Temperatures inside cone sacks should not exceed 25° C
	Should provide protection against predation

References

Barner, H. and Willan, R.L. 1985. Seed collection units: 1. Seed zones. Technical Notes No. 16. Danida Forest Seed Centre. Denmark.

Bramlett,D.L. (1974). Seed potential and seed efficiency. In: John Kraus; ed. Collloquium Proceedings, Seed yield from southern pine seed orchards. Macon GA: Georgia Forest Research Council. 7p.

Bramlett, D.L., Belcher, E.W., De Barr, G.L., Hertel, G.D., Karrfalt, R.P., Lantz, C.W., Miller,

T., Ware, K.D. and Yates, H.O. (1977): Cone analysis of southern pines - a guidebook. USDA Forest Service General Technical Report, Southern Forest Experiment Station No. SE-13, 28 pp.

El-Kassaby, Y., J. Maze, D. MacLeod, and S. Banerjee. 1991. Reproductive-cycle plasticity in

Howland, P. and Bowen, M.R. (1977): Triplochiton scleroxylon K. Schum., and other West African tropical hardwoods. West African Hardwoods Improvement Project research report, 1971–77. For. Res. Inst. of Nigeria, 154 pp.

IBPGR (1981): Report of first meeting, IBPGR Ad hoc Advisory Committee on Seed Storage, Kew, U.K., 10–11 Sept. 1981.

Keiding, H. (1973): Report on a journey to Sumatra, Thailand and India for the Danish/FAO Forest Tree Seed Centre, Jan. – March 1970. In Forest Genetic Resources Information No. 1. FAO Rome.

Kemp, R.H. (1973): Central American pine research project. In Forest Genetic Resources Information No. 1. FAO Rome.

Kemp, R.H. (1975 a): Seed collection: temporary storage and transport, documentation, training, safety and supervision. In Report on FAO/DANIDA Training Course on Forest Seed Collection and Handling, Vol. II. FAO Rome.

Poulsen, K. and Thomsen, K. (1999). Seed Handling Manual. Technical Note 54. Danida Forest Seed Centre. Denmark.

Purnomo, H. 1996. Seed information system (SIS). Ministry of Forestry, Directorate General of Reforestation and Land Rehabilitation, Indonesia Tree Seed Source Development Project. Danagro Adviser A/S.

Rasmussen, P. (1992). A guide to the NTSP seed documentation system, forms, rou-tines, files, source and accession numbers. National Tree Seed Project, Morogoro, Tanzania.

Seal, D.T., Matthews, J.D. and Wheeler, R.T. (1965): Collection of cones from standing trees For.. Record No. 39. For. Commission, London.

Stein, W.I., Slabaugh, P.E. and Plummer, A.P. (1974): Harvesting, processing and storage of fruits and seeds. In Seeds of Woody Plants in the United States, Agriculture Handbook No. 450. For. Service, USDA, Washington D.C98-125.

Turnbull, J.W. (1975 b): Seed collection - sampling considerations and collection techniques. In Report on FAO/DANIDA Training Course on Forest Seed Collection and Handling, Vol. 2, FAO Rome.

Turnbull, J.W. (1975 e): Seed collection of eucalypts. In Report on FAO/DANIDA Training Course on Forest Seed Collection and Handling, Vol. 2, FAO Rome.

Willcocks, K.W. (1974): Mobile elevating work platform. Aust. For. Ind. Journ. 40 (8): 33.

Zobel, D.B. 1979. Seed production in forests of Chamaecyparis lawsoniana. Can. J. For. Res. 9:327–35.

3

Extraction and Processing of Seed

The decision whether to extract the seed from the fruit at a central seed processing depot or close to the site of, and soon after, collection must be made in the light of local conditions. The reduction in bulk and weight of the collected material greatly facilitates transport and for this reason the extraction of the seed from relatively bulky fruits may be desirable at the site close to the collection area. In some cases it has also been found that early extraction of the seed is essential to maintain maximum viability. The use of the sun drying to speed extraction of the seed is common for many conifers and trees with woody dehiscent fruits. However, too rapid drying of fruits may sometimes cause them to remain closed and prevent later extraction, a condition known as "case-hardening" of cones. This is true for the cones of some pines if they are collected before peak maturity. In such cases it is necessary to keep the fruits under cover, with a good circulation of air, for one or two weeks before more rapid drying is attempted. Factors to be considered when deciding whether to extract seeds locally or centrally include:

- Distance to central seed processing depot and efficiency of the transport system. The longer the period to be spent in transit, the greater is the risk of deterioration.
- The characteristics of the species in question. For example, in fleshy fruits with a high risk of fermentation, seed should be extracted by maceration locally and soon after collection, while dry and resistant fruits and seeds of some leguminous species can withstand a lengthy transit period under poor conditions without serious loss of viability.
- The suitability of the species for extraction by sun. for example species which need kiln treatment for full extraction of the seeds will usually be sent to the central kiln-drying facilities without any attempt at local drying, but use of portable kilns or artificial heat from sawmills is sometimes feasible. Recalcitrant species which will not withstand drying are best dispatched moist to the central seed depot as soon as possible.

- The reliability of sunshine during the collection season. For instance dry and sunny weather will ensure ideal conditions for extraction of seed close to the area of collection. Similarly, in wet and cool-temperate conditions, sun drying is not practicable.
- When seed extraction is done locally, it is preferable to do it only if adequate facilities are available near the forest. The inaccessible and sparsely inhabited forests will have no such facilities and seed extraction can be performed only in central seed processing depot's.

Seed transportation

It is important to ensure that the minimum possible time should elapse between the dispatch of fruits or extracted seed from the collecting site or local seed collecting depot and its arrival at the central seed processing depot. Part of the planning operation is must to provide transport which is adequate in quantity and quality to avoid delays in dispatch and breakdowns en route. Even short stop-over can add to the heat build-up in fruit and cone sacks during transit. Railway transport is more economical over long distances. If distance to central seed processing depot is short and large quantities of seeds of a single species or provenance are to be transported, fruits may be loaded into vehicles without containers. The vehicle must be cleaned of all seed carried on previous trips before a new lot is loaded. For longer journeys or smaller seed lots individual containers should be used. Sacks should be carefully arranged in the vehicle to allow as much air circulation as possible between them.

To prevent excessive drying of these seeds the use of polythene bags and provision of shade against insulation are necessary. Transportation of seeds to the final destination immediately after collection may be essential for some species, which either germinate naturally or lose their viability soon after seed fall at normal temperatures. Provision of special insulated containers may thus be needed to control temperature and humidity during transit. Styrofoam containers or metal thermos flasks are recommended as a precaution against temporary exposure of recalcitrant seeds to cold or freezing conditions in aircraft holds (IBPGR 1981). With valuable collections it may be advisable to split each lot of seed or fruits to travel separately in order to guard against losing an entire collection through accidents en route. It may also be desirable to insure the contents against loss or damage, for a sum that will cover at least a proportion of the cost of repeating the collection.

Methods of seed extraction

The methods of extracting seeds from fruits or cones are determined mainly by their characteristics. Fleshy fruits are treated by a depulping process which usually involves a combination of soaking in water with pressure or gentle abrasion. Cones and other woody or leathery fruits are first dried until cone scales open or seeds become detached from the placenta of the fruit, and then treated manually or mechanically by tumbling or threshing in order to separate the dry seeds from the dry fruits. Some indehiscent fruits, mainly nuts, achenes and winged samaras, do not require extraction but are stored or sown as fruits. Some species with seeds covered by a thin fleshy covering may be dried and sown with the dried skin intact (Stein *et al.* 1974). Drying under cover with frequent turning of the fruits is appropriate. Examples are Vitex parviflora in the Philippines (Seeber and Agpaoa 1976), Crataegus in temperate regions (Goor and Barney 1976) and Podocarpus spp. and Maesopsis eminii in Africa.

Extraction of seeds from cones

Seeds of most conifers (Douglas-fir, larch, western redcedar, western hemlock, etc.) are obtained by drying cones to open them, shaking out the seeds, separating the seeds from cone scales and debris, then loosening the seed wings, and finally separating clean full seeds from wings, dust, empty seeds, and other small particles. Cedrus seed should be stored in the cones, since extracted seeds may lose their viability (Goor and Barney 1976). When removed from storage, the cones must be soaked in water to facilitate extraction. After treatment the cones can be easily broken apart by hand and the seeds extracted for immediate sowing.

Immature green cones may also need special treatment. It was found that green cones of Pinus merkusii from Zambales (Philippines), after soaking for 48 hours, followed by 80 hours' drying at a starting temperature of 30° C and a final temperature of 50° C, released only 7 % of the contained seeds; if the cycle of alternate soaking and drying was repeated 5 or 6 times, 79 % of seeds were released (Gordon *et al.* 1972). The total period of 4-5 weeks would be uneconomic in operational forestry. The recommended alternative is to collect only ripe brown cones, which released 91 % of their seeds in a single cycle.

Dewinging

Dry dewinging, a technique, which employs a rubbing action to remove wings from dry seed, is generally used for Douglas fir, pines, and true firs. Small lots can be dewinged in a cloth bag; lots of up to 5 kg are better handled in a Dybvig macerator (Belcher and Karrfalt, 1978); and large lots are best dewinged with a brush-type dewinger, although auger-type dewingers have also been used successfully. Because dry dewinging is the processing step that is most likely to cause seed damage, extra caution should be exercised to use proper equipment and to minimize unnecessary friction. In one study, for example, three cycles of brush dewinging seeds of subalpine fir [Abies lasiocarpa (Hook.) Nutt.] destroyed 50% of the originally viable seeds (Edwards, 1982). The principle of wet dewinging is that wings are more hygroscopic than seed and, upon wetting, are released cleanly. The Kason Vibrator (Edwards, 1981) and a rotating cement mixer with a soft brush (Wang, 1973) have been successfully used for wet dewinging. However, because seed absorbs moisture during wet dewinging, it must be redried sufficiently before storage. Germination tests verified that a 20 to 30 minute water soak, followed by wet dewinging and air drying for 16 hours at 26 to 30°C to 4 to 8% moisture content, did not adversely affect seed quality (Wang, 1973).

Cleaning

Seed material collected contains dust, stones, dirt, small debris and empty seed. The objective is to select a series of operations that will provide maximum production of high quality seed. The first step is to remove the debris with a screen cleaner. A laboratory model will adequately handle 50 to 100 pounds per hour (Banton 1946), which is adequate for most tree improvement work. The average inventory is better handled on a medium size, four- screen cleaner. The cleaner should remove large particles with the top screen while seed and small debris pass through. The first fan will remove dust and light debris. If long debris tends to go through the top screen, fasten a piece of plastic or plastic-coated cloth over one-fourth of the top screen. The cloth will keep the debris flat on the screen. Also, covering the lower part of the top screen will help improve separations when debris drops through too soon. Efficient accomplishment requires a positive and even feed to minimize the over and under-use and take the most advantage of air separation. Seed from the screen cleaner should be about 99 percent clean by visual observation. If the second air fan is properly set, most of the empty seed will be removed. With the move toward improved seed however, there has been a tendency to hold a few more empty or partly filled seed to avoid discarding any of the valuable seeds. This practice can lead to quicker seed deterioration in storage (Belcher and McConnell, 1974).

Upgrading seed

Even the best processing operation may not provide the desired seed quality. A continuous flow operation must process seed based on the average condition of the seed rather than the variation within the lot. Also, after periods of storage, deterioration may have reduced the seed viability to an unacceptable level. These problem lots are normally recognized after a seed test has been made. Low viability is the first sign of need for upgrading. First, a determination must be made of what to remove and then how to remove it. Removal of debris such as resin balls from white pine may require the use of an inclined draper. Some debris can be removed with a screen cleaner by changing screens. Slotted holes or triangular holes may be more effective than round holes.Partly filled seed and dead filled seed are the most difficult to remove, but if not removed they pose a source of further deterioration. The effort spent on this type of removal will depend on financial considerations. Improvements in separation require a gravity separator and a method to obtain density differences between living and dead seed.

Seed production in conifers

Before conducting seed production studies in natural stands, data should be collected on the below listed tree and stand characteristics known to influence natural seed production (Alexander *et al.,* 1986):

- Density (number of seed trees per hectare).
- Spatial arrangement of seed trees.
- Age of seed trees.
- Evidence of past production.
- Evidence of animal use (e.g., squirrel caches)
- Total height to the nearest 0.15 m.
- Diameter at breast height (dbh).
- Assessments of the general health and vigour of the crowns.
- Average length of live crown
- Basal area values of all trees with dbh of 25.4 cm and larger may be included because trees of this size probably would be sufficiently mature to produce seeds (McCaughey and Schmidt 1987).

References

Banton, Ronald. Problems in cleaning seed. (1946). Saginaw, MI: A. T. Ferrell & Co.; 12p.

Belcher, E. W., Jr., and R. P. Karrfalt. 1978. The processing of conifer seed. Pages 9-18 in Proc., Small lot forest seed processing workshop. U.S.D.A. Forest Serv. Southeastern Area, State and Private Forestry.

Belcher, E W.; McConnell, J. L., (1974). Nineteenth Report, Eastern Tree Seed Laboratory, fiscal years 1973 and 1974, Macon, GA: U.S. Department of Agriculture, Forest Service, Southeastern Area;, 16p.

Edwards, D. G. W. 1981. Cone collection and processing. Effects on seed quality and yield. Pages 12-37 in Proc.. High-quality collection and production of conifer seed. Northern Forest Res. Centre, Edmonton. Inf. Rep. NOR-X-235.

Goor, A.Y. and Barney, C.W. (1976): Forest tree planting in arid zones (2nd Ed.). Ronald Press, New York.

Gordon, A.G., Estaban, I.D. and Wakeman, D.C. (1972): Cone handling, seed quality and seed testing of Pinus merkusii. Commonw. For. Rev. 51 (1), 70–75.

IBPGR (1981): Report of first meeting, IBPGR Ad hoc Advisory Committee on Seed Storage, Kew, U.K., 10–11 Sept. 1981.

ISAACS, W.J. (1972): What is the latest in cone and seed handling equipment and techniques? Proc. S.E. Area For. Tree Nurserymen's Conf. Mississippi and N. Carolina: 228–231.

Seeber, G. and Agpaoa, A. (1976): Forest Tree Seeds. In Manual of Reforestation and Erosion Control for the Philippines, 473–535. German Agency for Technical Co-operation, Eschborn.

Stein, W.I., Slabaugh, P.E. and Plummer, A.P. (1974): Harvesting, processing and storage of fruits and seeds. In Seeds of Woody Plants in the United States, Agriculture Handbook No. 450. For. Service, USDA, Washington D.C.

Wang, B. S. P. 1973. Collecting, processing and storing tree seed for research use. Proc., IUFRO International symp. on seed processing. Bergen, Norway. Vol. I, Pap. 17. 12 p.

4

Seed Dormancy and Germination

Seed dormancy

Plants evolve many mechanisms that ensure their survival. For instance, some species produce prodigious number of seeds so that even if only a small proportion germinate and grow, some seedlings will survive. Alternately, dormancy can be defined as: a seed characteristic, the degree of which defines what conditions should be met to make the seed germinate. This definition may be more useful in understanding dormancy because it suggests that dormancy is variable, rather than constant, which is the situation that we generally encounter in the native populations of many species. The staggering of germination (dormancy) is an advantage for seeds that mature in late summer to early fall, since immediate germination would leave vulnerable seedlings exposed to harsh winter conditions.

Variation in dormancy

Woody species vary tremendously in their degree of dormancy which is either genetically controlled (Edwards and El-Kassaby 1995). The strategies of dormancy may differ according to the characteristics and the timing of critical events of individual life cycles. For example, long- lived species such as pines, which require almost three years from cone bud initiation to seed maturation, would not be expected to have the same dormancy characteristics as small herbaceous annuals that germinate, flower, and set seed within three months. Climatic factors play a crucial role in controlling the length of dormancy. For instance a seed of a sacred lotus (Nelumbo nucifera) dated at about 1,300 years and one of a date palm about 2,000 years old found in Israel and China have sucessessfully germinated under unfavourable environmental conditions (Shen-Miller, 1995).

Seed scientist has devised many different classifications of dormancy. One of these classifications has recognized three types of seed dormancy viz. primary, secondary (induced) and enforced. Primary dormancy occurs during seed maturation and the seed does not germinate readily upon being shed. Secondary and enforced conditions caused by adverse environmental factors such as high or low temperature, absence of oxygen or light, low soil moisture and the presence of chemical inhibitors. Seeds with secondary dormancy, e.g mountain ash (Sorbus spp.) apple, box (Buxus spp.), Tartarian maple (Acer tartaricum), and European spindle tree (Euonymus europea); need additional environmental stimuli to germinate spontaneously even when environmental conditions improve. Phytochrome imparts to the seed the ability to interpret light quality and to distinguish light from dark with respect to its position in the soil.

A detailed classification of seed dormancy has been given by Gordon and Rowe (1982). The system is hierarchical with these five classes further divided into levels and types Baskin and Baskin (2004).

Exogenous dormancy (seed coat dormancy)

i. Physical i.e. impermeability of seed coat or pericarp to water
ii. Chemical i.e. inhibitors in pericarp or seed coat
iii. Mechanical i.e. Mechanical resistance of pericarp or seed coat to embryo growth

Endogenous dormancy (morphological dormancy)

iv. Morphological i.e. underdevelopment of embryo

Endogenous dormancy (physiological dormancy)

v. Physiological i.e. germination prevented by physiological inhibiting mechanism
vi. Shallow i.e. Inhibiting mechanism weak
vii. Intermediate i.e. Inhibiting mechanism intermediate
viii. Deep i.e. Inhibiting mechanism strong

Combined morpho-physiological dormancy

i. Combination of underdevelopment of embryo with strong physiological inhibiting
ii. Combination of underdevelopment of embryo with strong physiological inhibiting mechanism.

Combined exogenous/endogenous dormancy

i. Various combinations of seedcoat or pericarp dormancy with endogenous physiological dormancy e.g. Tilia cordata combines physical impermeability of the seedcoat with deep physiological dormancy.

Exogenous or Seed coat dormancy

This type of dormancy has three primary modes of action. In most common mode, the seed coats are impermeable to the entry of moisture or gas. Members of Leguminoseae- for example Acacia, Albizia, honeylocust, blacklocust, Melilotus and Trigonella (both Fabaceae) etc usually display this character, which is commonly called hard seededness. The second mode of dormancy action can be attributed to seed coats is the mechanical resistance to swelling of embryo as it absorbs moisture. This resistance delays full imbibition and emergence of radicle from within the seed. This type of dormancy is reported to occur in sagebrush (Artemesia tridentate Nutt.) (McDonough and Harnis, 1974), pecan (Van Staden and Dimalla, 1976) and lobloby pine (Baenett, 1976). The possible mode of seed coat dormancy is the presence of germination inhibitors in the seed coats that may or may not play a significant role in dormancy. Some of the phenolic substances in the seed coats that may possibily be germination inhibitors could actually be beneficial by inhibiting the growth of pathogenic micro-organisms (Mohamed- Yaseen *et al.*, 1994).

Treatments designed to break exogenous or Seed coat dormancy

Seeds of some species have hard, cutinised seed coats that completely prevent the imbibition of water and sometimes also the exchange of gases. Without imbibition and gas exchange renewal of embryo growth and germination are impossible. Physical seed coat dormancy of this kind occurs most frequently in species adapted to alternating dry and wet seasons, including several leguminous genera such as Acacia, Prosopis, Ceratonia, Robinia, Albizzia and Cassia. In some species, e.g. Tectona grandis and Pterocarpus angolensis, the hard layer is formed by the pericarp or fruit. The unit of dispersal, storage and sowing in Tectona often referred to loosely as the "seed" is the fruit, but for practical purposes the origin of the impermeable layer does not affect the choice of pretreatment.

Chemical seed coat dormancy caused by the presence of chemicals located in the seed coat can usually be overcomed by some form of liquid treatment which leaches out the chemicals. The wet treatment methods described in this chapter should therefore be effective in breaking chemical and physical seed coat dormancy and as well as a combination of the two. Dry methods on the other hand, which are effective in overcoming physical dormancy, are unlikely to have any effect on chemical dormancy.

Physical methods

One of the simplest and most direct physical methods is to cut, drill or file a small hole in the coat of each seed before sowing (Goor and Barney 1976).

This method has been found appropriate for large leguminous seeds in the genera Afzelia, Albizzia, Intsia and Sindora (Seeber and Agpaoa 1976) and for Acacia, Prosopis, Enterolobium and other legumes (Robbins 1982 b). Seed is nicked at each end in the area of the hilum and micropyle. In Tanzania the hard and bristly pericarp of Pterocarpus angolensis is chipped at one edge by knife (Laurie 1974) or cracked by beating with clubs (Boaler 1966). In the Philippines the hard seed coat of Eusideroxylon is cracked by hammer. In Calophyllum complete removal of the seedcoat has produced better germination than nicking (Seeber and Agpaoa 1976). Sand paper may also be used to reduce seed coat thickness by abrasion. The effect of physical scarification may be reinforced by soaking in cold water before sowing.

For treatment of large quantities of seed, mechanical scarification (Fig 1)is more suitable than the manual method. Seeds may be tumbled or churned in a concrete mixer with sharp gravel or sand, or in a special drum lined with abrasive material such as sandpaper, cement or crushed glass or incorporating rotating abrasive disks. If gravel or sand is used, it should be sieved to ensure that it can be readily separated from the seed by use of an appropriate mesh screen. The method is not suitable for seeds with abundant resin or pulp that may clog the machine. Care must be taken to avoid over treatment causing damage that can reduce or destroy germinability of the seeds. Examination of the seedcoat surface by hand lens, or testing the capacity of the seed to take up water; demonstrated by swelling, can be used to estimate effectiveness of scarification (Bonner *et al.* 1974). In India mechanical scarification is used successfully to overcome seedcoat dormancy in *Acacia catechu, A. nilotica subsp. indica, Albizzia falcataria, A. lebbek, Cassia fistula, C. javanica, C. nodosa, Delonix regia, Dichrostachys cinerea, Santalum album, Terminalia arjuna and T. tomentosa* (Pattanath 1982).

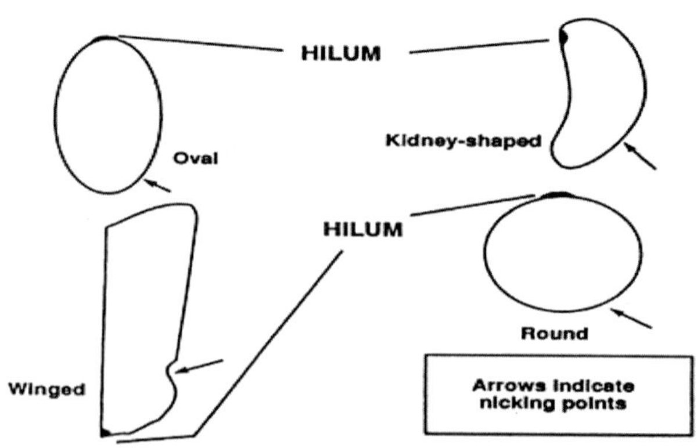

Fig. 1. Scarification points by seed shape.

Soaking in water

Some seeds which have little resistance to germination may respond well to soaking for 24 hours in water at ambient temperature. In India soaking in water, for periods varying from two to 48 hours according to species, accelerates germination in *Acacia mearnsii, A. melanoxylon, A. nilotica subsp. kraussiana, Adenanthera microsperma, Albizzia amara, A. procera, Grevillea robusta* and *Trewia nudiflora* (Pattanath 1982).

Alternate wetting and drying

A more effective treatment, especially in hot climates, is alternate wetting and drying of seed. This has frequently been used for *Tectona* fruits. Bryndum (1966) has recommended alternate soaking and drying (4 times soaking and 3 times drying, each for 30-45 minutes) after scarification for improved results. If preliminary scarification is not applied, common practice is to spread the "seed" on a hard surface in the sun in a layer about 5 cm deep and to soak it thoroughly; then to turn it over from time to time to allow it to dry out and bake in the sun for a day or two. This process of alternate soaking, drying and baking is repeated a number of times, usually between five and ten cycles, until signs of germination appear. Each cycle of wetting and drying may be one day for soaking and 3-5 days for drying and baking. As soon as germination starts, the "seed" should be sown in the nursery (Laurie 1974).

Hot water treatment

The seeds are usually placed into boiling water which is immediately removed from the heat source and left to cool for about 12 hours. They imbibe and swell as the water cools. The proper relationship of the volume of water to volume of seeds can be determined by experiment. It may vary considerably according to species, ratios of 2 – 3 times (Goor and Barney 1976), 4 – 5 times (Bonner *et al.* 1974) and 5 –10 times (Seeber and Agpaoa 1976) as much water as seed have been suggested. Some species respond better to an initial temperature well below boiling e.g. Albizzia falcataria (Valencia 1973). An initial temperature of 90° C, cooled to ambient 20° C, has given good results with Parkinsonia aculeata and Ziziphus spina-christi (Kisou *et al.* 1983).

Prescriptions for hot water treatment must be applied meticulously if seed coat dormancy is to be removed without killing the seeds through excessive heating. It is often easier to ensure this at a central research laboratory than in a number of scattered field nurseries. In Sabah it was found possible to redry seeds of Acacia mangium and Albizzia falcataria after the initial 30 seconds' hot water treatment, package and despatch them to field nurseries and after a 3 days' storage give a simple cold water soak before sowing. Hot water treatment is relatively easy and safe to apply, as well as being effective with some species; however, it is not well adapted to large lots because of the difficulty in handling and sowing the swollen seeds (Heit 1967).

Acid treatment

Great care is needed in the handling of sulfuric acid and this method is not suitable for use by unskilled workers. The optimum period of immersion in acid for each lot may be determined by treating a small sample for different periods and then soaking the lots in water at room temperature for 1 to 5 days (depending on species). The treatment period that yields a high percentage of swollen seeds (by water uptake) without visible injury is the right one. Oversoaking may pit the seed and even expose the endosperm. Insufficient soaking leaves the seedcoats of most species glossy and the coats of correctly treated seeds are dull but not deeply pitted (Fig 2).

Precautions for use of sulfuric acid

- All workmen must understand and obey safety precautions while using an acid. They should wear suitable safety clothing, gloves, and goggles or other eye protection.
- Seeds, containers, implements and the acid itself must be handled with great care to avoid injury.
- Water must not be splashed into the acid, as a violent reaction will occur.

The steps in acid treatment are

1. Allow seeds to come to air temperature. If they have been removed from cold storage do not open the container until temperature equilibrium is reached. Moisture will form on cold seeds exposed to warm moist air and this moisture can react with acid to raise temperature to the danger point.
2. Mix seeds thoroughly to be treated as one lot.
3. Immerse seeds in the acid for the required period, making sure that all are covered.
4. Treatment should be carried out at 65° to 80° F (18°–27°C). Temperatures below this range will require longer soaking times. Careful stirring will reduce the length of treatment necessary.
5. Remove seeds from the acid and wash them promptly and thoroughly in cool, running water for 5 to 10 minutes to remove all traces of acid. Water should be applied copiously at the start and the seeds stirred carefully during rinsing.

a) Treatment of large lots of seed treated with acid. (USDA Forest Service)

b) A rinsing trough for washing acid from seeds. (USDA Forest Service)

Fig. 2. Treatment of seeds with acid

Biological methods

In nature animals and microorganisms are an important factor in the breakdown of seedcoat impermeability. It is difficult to make use of these organisms as a controlled pretreatment of seed, but in a few cases successful results have been obtained. Seeds of Acacia senegal and *Ceratonia siliqua* that have passed through the digestive tracts of goats germinate readily when placed in favourable conditions (Goor and Barney 1976).

Termites are an important agent for breaking down seed coat dormancy in many parts of the tropics. In Thailand teak fruits are spread on the ground in a 5 cm thick layer immediately after collection and covered with cardboard and in about 5 weeks the termites remove the exocarp to facilitate easy germination. Periodic inspection is essential to ensure that the process is not carried too far.

Partial fermentation, which is damaging to many seeds, can be beneficial in overcoming seedcoat dormancy. In the southern Sudan fruits of *Tectona grandis* are allowed to lie on the ground through the rainy season for partial fermentation (Wunder 1966). They are then collected, stratified in a pit with layers of (a) Seed (b) Organic matter (c) Soil and watered daily for 10 days.

Dry heat and fire

In wet and dry tropics, fire is a powerful natural factor in the removal of seed coat dormancy. A fierce fire will kill the seeds but a light to moderate fire, such as those associated with controlled burning will reduce seedcoat impermeability and stimulate germination. The fruits are spread thickly on the ground and covered with grass which is burnt off. Adjusting the heat of the fire to achieve the maximum effect on the pericarp without damaging the seed embryo requires experience. In Sabah Bowen and Eusebio (1981) found that ten minutes' exposure of Acacia mangium seeds to dry heat at 100° C was nearly as effective in overcoming dormancy as the immersion in water at 100°C.

Special treatments for mechanical dormancy

The thick, tough but water-permeable coverings of seeds exhibiting mechanical dormancy prevent embryo growth even when water can be freely imbibed. This mechanical obstruction to germination can be overcomed by a period of "warm moist" treatment, the length of which varies according to species. The treatment recommended by Gordon and Rowe (1982) for temperate species is:

- Soak seeds in several times their volume of cold water at approximately 3–5°C for 48 hours.
- Drain off the water and mix the seeds with (two to four times their volume) water-retaining medium such as sand, sand/peat mixture or vermiculite.
- Store at a warm temperature. A constant 20–25°C or alternating 20° and 30°C is suitable for many species.
- Open containers weekly, mix seeds and if surfaces show signs of drying out remoisten with water spray.

The period of "warm moist" treatment can be shortened in some species by a preliminary treatment in sulfuric acid. This requires more care and expertise than the use of acid for physical dormancy. Seeds or fruits must be thoroughly dried before treatment and the process should be limited to the partial digestion of the outer layers only, leaving the final weakening of the inner layers to be done by the subsequent warm moist treatment. Periods of treatment vary from 2 weeks for some species of *Prunus* to 16 weeks for some species of *Crataegus*.

Treatments designed to break morphological and physiological dormancy

Embryo dormancy is a prominent feature in both orthodox and recalcitrant seeds. Endogenous dormancy includes the cases of embryos which are morphologically underdeveloped at the time of separation from the parent tree and which need a subsequent period for further growth before they can germinate. It also includes the cases of embryos which are morphologically mature at the time of seed dispersal or collection but physiologically incapable of germination until certain biochemical changes, still little understood, take place.

Morphological dormancy

Seeds with underdeveloped embryos at the time of dispersal or collection will not germinate until the embryos have had time to mature. In a few species maturation is possible during dry storage e.g. Gingko biloba (Hatano and Kano 1952). More commonly, a period of moist warm pretreatment is necessary before the embryos develop sufficiently for germination to take place. The recommended treatment (Gordon and Rowe 1982) is the same as described above.

Physiological dormancy

Far more common than morphological dormancy among temperate species are the cases where seeds are fully developed at dispersal or collection but are inhibited from immediate germination for physiological reasons. The pretreatment most effective in removing this physiological dormancy is that which approximates to the conditions of over wintering in nature i.e. a moist cold treatment or cold stratification which is a method of placing seeds in layers alternating with layers of a moisture-retaining medium such as sand, peat or vermiculite, and keeping them at a cool temperature for a period that varies by species and handling techniques. The three main requirements for success in stratification and moist prechilling are a renewable source of moisture for the seeds, low temperature and adequate aeration. Only imbibed seeds will benefit fully from cold, moist treatment, while good aeration is needed to supply oxygen for respiration and to dissipate heat and CO_2. Low temperature not only favour biochemical changes in the seed but also reduces micro-organism activity and the risk of overheating and premature germination of the after-ripened seeds (Bonner *et al.* 1974). Periods of prechilling vary considerably from species to species and, to some extent, from seed lot to seed lot within a species (Aldhous 1972). A prime example of the latter is eastern white pine, which usually requires 30 to 60 days for stratification. Most studies at the National Tree Seed Laboratory show that at least 21 days are required for stratification to be effective on slash and loblolly pine seed. For Acer macrophyllum, this is about 60 to 120 days (J. Zasada, pers. comm. 1996). This increase in the length of stratification has been found to increase the speed of germination (USDA, 1974).

Cold stratification simulates winter conditions by exposing moist seeds to cold temperatures. The treatment not only overcome physiological dormancy but also reduces the sensitivity of both dormant and non-dormant seeds to their optimum requirements for light and temperature, resulting in increased rate and uniformity of germination over a variety of conditions. This treatment allows monitoring the condition of the seeds throughout the prechilling operation and there is no need to separate seeds from medium at the end of treatment. Naked" prechilling is satisfactory for species which need only a few weeks' prechilling, while use of a medium is advisable for those which need a longer prechilling period and for all species which need warm moist pretreatment.

Traditional stratification techniques may be insufficient to stimulate germination in some conifer species. The true firs (amabilis, grand, noble, and subalpine) respond best to a two-part stratification called stratification-redry (Leadem, 1989). Abies seeds that receive the stratification-redry treatment are able to germinate more quickly and more completely. For the stratification-redry treatment, seeds are hydrated for 48 h and then stratified for 4 weeks at 2°C to 5°C; seed mc is high, usually above 40%. The seeds are then dried to 25-30 °C mc and chilled for an additional 12 weeks. Moisture is a critical factor in the application of the stratification-redry treatment. The stratification-redry treatment has also been found effective for some sources of Douglas-fir seeds, but not for other tree species, perhaps because the correct redry me has not been found.

A variation of the preceding method is the compound stratification treatment used for Pinus monticola and for immature seeds. The treatment is referred to as compound stratification because the seeds are exposed to both warm and cold temperatures. The usual combination used for Pinus monticola is 30 days "warm" stratification (20°C to 25°C) followed by 60 days "cold" stratification (2°C to 5°C). However, the duration of warm stratification may vary, depending upon the seed source. Thus, seeds are kept under warm conditions until about 5% of the seeds show evidence of germination, and then they are transferred to cold temperatures (D.W.G. Edwards pers. comm. 1996). Compound stratification also works well on Chamaecyparis nootkatensis. This treatment is similar to "stratification -redry" treatments described above and involves hydrating the seeds to a predetermined mc ("Y"), depending on the species, then chilling the seeds at this mc for X+2 weeks. The duration of treatment (expressed in weeks), is represented as "X", or the time when 10% of the seeds have germinated. This length of stratification is sufficient to break dormancy, but germination is prevented because moisture levels are controlled during the chilling period. After treatment, the seeds can either be sown, or re-dried to below 10% mc and stored for several years (Muller and Bonnet-Masimbert 1989; Muller *et al.* 1990). They can be sown at any time and they will germinate readily as they are no longer dormant. This dormancybreaking treatment is usually applied after storage, but it can also be applied before storage, i.e., immediately after collection. The time period "X" can be considered to be an indication of the degree of seed dormancy, and potentially could be used to compare the dormancy levels of different seed sources. The period "X" is 1 to 3 months for beechnuts (Fagus sylvatica), 5 to 6 months for wild cherries, (Prunus sativum), and 6 to 8 months for ash (Fraxinus spp.) (Suszka *et al.*, 1996).

The main features of stratification are:

- The size of the pit is adjusted according to the volume of seed to be stratified.
- The pit should be located in a cool, shady and well-drained site.
- The bottom 10 cm should be filled with either sand or gravel for drainage.
- Pit contents should remain moist during stratification, but should never become waterlogged.
- Dry seeds cannot be stratified. They must be imbibed before stratification.

Procedure for stratification in plastic bags

i. Bring seeds to a high moisture content. Full imbibition is essential for stratification in plastic bags without a moisture-holding medium. The usual procedure is to soak the seeds overnight at room temperature; then drain them for several minutes over wire screens.

ii. Place seeds loosely in bags (4 mils thick); do not pack. Close the bags tightly to prevent loss of moisture.

iii. Label all containers clearly, and place them in the cooling facility. (36 to 38 °F).

iv. Inspect bags periodically. Poor aeration is more of a problem in naked stratification than it is when a medium is used, especially for large lots. There is some gas exchange through the bag walls, but frequent inspections and turnings are necessary. One easy means of detecting a lack of oxygen is to open the bags and smell the contents. An odor of alcohol indicates that anaerobic respiration is occurring because of insufficient oxygen. A faint smell of alcohol does not mean that the seeds are ruined, but it serves as a warning of imminent danger. Inspect the bags more often than weekly if you have large lots, and open and turn all bags.

v. Remove and wash the seeds at the end of the stratification period. Washing at this point may not be necessary, but it will remove some potentially damaging microorganisms, especially with large hardwood seeds. Sowing soon after removal is recommended as for any stratification procedure.

Chemical treatment of physiological dormancy

Dormancy-breaking treatments have been shown to greatly affect the concentration of a number of plant hormones within the seed. In addition, applications of hormones to whole seeds and excised embryos have been shown to influence their dormancy status. Consequently, hormones are thought to be intimately involved in, and even to control, seed dormancy. They include gibberellic acid, citric acid, ethephon, hydrogen peroxide and a number of other compounds. The application of hormones to whole seeds and embryos influences their dormancy status. In general chemical treatments cannot compete with stratification or moist prechilling in deeply dormant seeds, but can reduce required treatment time.

Treatments designed to overcome double dormancy

Pretreatments to break one type of dormancy alone will be largely ineffective, unless it is followed by a second pre-treatment to overcome the other type. Physical dormancy of the seed coat may be combined with physiological dormancy of the embryo. In this case seedcoats should be treated first e.g. by scarification and cold moist prechilling applied afterwards to overcome embryo dormancy (Table 1).

Other treatments used for breaking seed dormancy

i. X-rays, gamma rays, light rays in the red region of the spectrum and high frequency sound waves have all been used experimentally to try to overcome dormancy and stimulate germination. Improvement has been reported in some species, but it has proved difficult to achieve consistent results and the treatments may induce chromosome damage and other abnormalities (Kemp, 1975).

ii. Invigoration and priming has been used to over come the dormancy of pine seeds (Bergsten, 1987). In this treatment the moisture available to the seed is limited. This is done either by imbibing seeds in osmotic solutions or by limiting the amount of water. The seeds are placed at germination temperatures of 15 to 20°C usually for periods up to two weeks. To improve the performance of seeds it is recommended that pre-chilling at controlled moisture content should be followed by invigoration at the same moisture content (Downie and Bergsten, 1991; Jones *et al.,* 1993).

iii. The addition of compost activator, such as Garotta to treatment medium has been found to influence the dormancy of woody seeds (Morpeth *et al.*, 1997).

Table 1. Effect of some important dormancy - release treatments for tree seeds.

Treatment	**Description**
Scarification	Chemical (sulphuric acid) or mechanical (abrasion) treatment: breaks down seed coats
Plant growth regulators	Enhance natural levels in favour of germination
High oxygen concentrations	Supply respiration; remove metabolic blocks
Leaching	Soaking in water; removes inhibitors from seed coats
Light	Exposure to specific wavelengths; stimulates the phytochrome system
Stratification	Moist chilling at 2-5°C; removes metabolic blocks, weakens seed coats, increases germination promoter levels

Hydration

Seed moisture content is an indicator of the physiological state of the seed. Moisture content can be used as a guide to determine whether seeds are in a condition suitable for stratification or sowing, or whether they can be stored or shipped without damage. When the moisture content of seed falls below 10 percent, the metabolic activity is virtually non-existent. Therefore seeds must be rehydrated fully before germination can proceed. This involves soaking the seeds in water or placing them in a highly humid environment. Dry seeds take up water rapidly but early hydration is essentially a passive process. The separation between the two categories is possible when seeds have rehydrated fully. Seeds are first soaked in water, kept at 15–25°C for several days to ensure that tissues are physiologically functional and then dried for a few hours (Table 2). During this drying low-vigour or damaged seeds lose their moisture more quickly than high vigour seeds. When the partially dried seeds are placed in water, low-vigour seeds tend to float, whereas high-vigour seeds tend to sink.

Table 2. Moisture content guidelines for tree seeds

Moisture content (%)	**Physiological status**
< 5	All water is chemically bound; removal may be detrimental
5 - 10	Seeds may be stored for prolonged periods at low temperature (- 18°C)
<20	Seeds may revert to dormant state
25 - 30	Reduced risk for premature germination during stratification (2-5°C)
30 – 45 +	Moisture level of fully imbibed seeds in preparation for stratification or sowing

Activation

Once the seeds are fully hydrated, moisture content and respiration remain relatively constant as the essential growth processes of germination take place. During this phase, physiological activity is high as stored reserves are mobilized, DNA (the genetic coding) is activated, and cell repair and cell division begin. The storage compounds broken down during respiration release their energy to drive the processes of germination. Other raw materials will be used to form proteins, membranes and other cellular structures of the developing seedling. At the end of activation cell elongation and radicle emergence occur - the first visible (outward) sign that germination has commenced.

Emergence

The embryo grows primarily through cell division and elongation of existing cells. Cell elongation is promoted by the transport of sugars, which increases the tendency of the embryo cells to take up water. The increased water pressure assists in the growth of the radicle, enabling it to break through the seed coat. Once the radicle emerges, water uptake resumes. Oxygen is now more readily available to the embryo and respiration rises sharply to supply the energy needs of the new seedling.

Factors influencing germination of seeds

Temperature

Plants may be classified into four groups with regard to the temperatures at which their seeds germinate: The first type is cool temperature tolerant species, which represent most plants that are native to temperate zones. Seed of cool temperature tolerant species can germinate at temperatures as low as 4.5° C (40 °F) but prefer optimal temperature in the range of 25°-30°C (77°-86 °F) for germination to occur. The second group of plants require cool temperatures for seed germination. Seeds of this type originate from cool season plants, most of which are native to the Mediterranean type climates. These climates usually have hot, dry summers and cool moist winters. In terms of seed germination, it is favorable for seed to germinate in winter under cool moist conditions rather than during the hot, dry summer. The third group of plants require warm temperatures for seed germination to take place. Seeds of this type generally will not germinate unless soil temperatures are 10-15°C (50°-60 °F) and show visible signs of chilling injury if germination at lower temperature occurs. Seedlings afflected with chilling injury may be chlorotic, slow growing and accompanied by disease problems. Most of these plants are tropical in origin and adapted to regions where soil temperatures do not get very low. The fourth group of plants require an alternating diurnal cycle of temperatures to initiate germinate. Basically, this involves alternating temperatures of warmth provided by sunlight during the day and cooling of soil at night through radiant heat loss.

Temperature is one of the most important factor affecting seeds. In nature, germination usually occurs over a range of temperatures that are higher during the day and lower at night. Thus a diurnal temperature is often used during germination tests. All seeds have an optimum temperature or temperature range for germination. A temperature regime of 30°C during the day (8-h light) and 20°C at night (16-h dark) is commonly used for most species. Tree seeds usually germinate more quickly under high temperatures. For example, although Pacific silver fir seeds usually germinate quickly under warm conditions (30°C days and 20°C nights), total germination is often greater when seeds are incubated under cool conditions (15°C days and 10°C nights). Such a positive response at low temperatures may reflect an adaption of true fir seeds to the cool environments they would ordinarily encounter in nature. Stratification broadens the temperature range for germination. Unstratified seeds tend to germinate well within a fairly narrow temperature range, but beyond that range germination may decline notably. It is impossible to predict what environmental conditions will exist when seeds are sown in forest nurseries. Stratification allows earlier sowing and more reliable germination under unfavourable early season temperatures.

Oxygen

Oxygen is required for respiration that fuels the germination process. Oxygen requirements differ by species but since most tree seeds are able to germinate at concentrations well below atmospheric levels (21% by volume). Oxygen is therefore not generally considered to be a limiting factor. In flooded soils, however, available oxygen can be limited because the air in soil pore spaces is displaced by water. Seed coats also act as barriers to oxygen during germination, as indicated by the marked increase in respiration after radicles protrude through the coat.

Light

Seeds require light to stimulate germination, but seeds must be fully hydrated in order to respond. The light stimulus is received through the phytochrome system, which operates as an on/off switch for many physiological processes in plants. Germination is usually stimulated by exposure to red light (660 nm) and inhibited by exposure to far-red light (730 nm). The light intensity of 1–5 lx (comparable to bright moonlight) is generally sufficient to activate the phytochrome system. Seeds lying on or near the soil surface receive enough light to trigger germination if all other conditions have been satisfied. However, seeds buried too deeply in the soil would not receive enough light for germination. In the nursery, the light requirement is generally met during routine handling of hydrated seeds. The light requirement for germination may be affected by treatments such as stratification. For example, un-stratified seeds of species that require light for germination can be made to germinate in darkness once they have been stratified.

Immaturity

Failure to germinate is not always linked to dormancy. Poor germination may be caused by immaturity i.e. seeds may have been picked too early or collected from high elevation or high latitude areas that experience shortened growing seasons. Such seeds may benefit from artificial ripening after they have been collected and before they are extracted.

Natural regeneration

The success of natural regeneration programs depends on how well seedbed environments meet the requirements for seed germination and seedling establishment. The suitability of different seedbeds varies with their light, moisture, and temperature characteristics. Many conifer seeds germinate better on mineral soils because they provide more available moisture and higher average temperatures than organic soils. However, in bright sunlight the surface temperatures of mineral soils can become so high as to be lethal to germinating seeds. Rotting wood can be a good substrate because it retains moisture well, whereas surfaces that have been burned tend to develop high temperatures that reduce the moisture-holding capability of upper soil layers. Seedbed environments can be enhanced by selecting appropriate silvicultural systems and site preparation methods. Site preparation can improve natural regeneration by increasing the amount of exposed mineral soil and by bringing buried seeds to the surface. Burning is probably detrimental to most conifer species since seeds are generally on or close to the surface of the forest floor and are therefore vulnerable to mortality from even a low severity fire.

Logging may affect seed germination by altering critical environmental variables. Total canopy removal may result in higher soil temperatures and extreme temperature fluctuations. In northern areas where moisture is not limiting, complete canopy removal is sometimes beneficial because soil temperatures at high elevations or northern exposures are often too cold for germination. The increased exposure of logged areas may stimulate the germination of species such as pines, but may inhibit the germination of species adapted to shaded habitats. Partial canopy removal may create more favourable conditions for germination because of the moderating influence of forest cover on light, moisture, and temperature conditions of the seedbed.

Slow rates of regeneration and forest regrowth after clearcut harvesting have stirred controversy about the sustainability of harvesting in subalpine forests (Farnden 1994; Vyse 1997). Slow rates of natural regeneration in large clearcuts coupled with other regeneration problems like presence of resin vesicles within the seed coat, deep physiological dormancy, presence of relatively high proportions of abnormal germinants, namely those with stunted radicles etc have plagued the successful germination of alpine and sub-alpine flora. All these factors have forced many silviculturists to dismiss natural regeneration on alpine and subalpine sites in favour of artificial regeneration. Improvements in artificial reforestation, including seedling stock types and site preparation, have increased regeneration success rates on clearcut-harvested subalpine sites. Nevertheless, the steady ingress of natural regeneration in harvested areas often contributes significantly to overall restocking, species diversity, and the spatial structure of regenerating stands. Current changes in harvest practices, including reductions in average clearcut size and increasing use of partial-cut silvicultural systems, may increase the use of natural regeneration opportunities on harvested subalpine forest sites.

References

Aldhous, J.R. (1972): Nursery practice. Forestry Comm. Bull. No. 43, London.

Baskin, C. C. and Baskin, J. M. (2004) A classification system forseed dormancy. Seed ScienceResearch 14, 1-16.

Boaler, S.B. (1966): The ecology of Pterocarpus angolensis D.C. in Tanzania. Overseas Res. Pub., Min. of Overseas Dev., London No. 12.

Bonner, F.T., McLemore, B.F. and Barnett, J.P. (1974): Presowing treatment of seed to speed germination. In Seeds of Woody Plants in the United States, Agriculture Handbook No. 450. For. Service, USDA, Washington D.C.

Bryndum, K. (1966): The germination of teak. Natural History Bull. Siam Society 21, 75–86.

Durzan DJ and Chalupa V. (1968). Free sugars, amino acids, and soluble proteins in the embryo and female gametophyte of jack pine as related to climate at the seed source. Canadian Journal of Botany 46: 417–428.

Goor, A.Y. and Barney, C.W. (1976): Forest tree planting in arid zones (2nd Ed.). Ronald Press, New York.

Gordon, A.G. and Rowe, D.C.F. (1982): Seed manual for ornamental trees and shrubs. For. Comm. Bull. 59, HMSO London.

Hatano, K. and Kano, T. (1952): A brief report on the after-ripening of the seeds of Gingko biloba. J. Jap. For. Soc. 34 : 369 – 370. Cited in Krugman et al. 1974.

Heit, C.E, (1967 a): Propagation from seed. Part 6: Hardseededness - a critical factor. Am. Nurseryman 125 (12).

Heit, C.E. (1967 b): Propagation from seed. Part 10: Storage methods for conifer seeds. Ammerican Nurseryman 126 (8).

Kemp, R.H. (1975): Seed pretreatment and principles of nursery handling. In Report on FAO/ DANIDA Training Course on Forest Seed Collection and Handling, Vol. II. FAO Rome.

Kisou, J., Khazraji, S. and Back G. (1983): Ten exercises in testing of forest tree seeds. Institutionen för skogsskötsel, Sveriges Lantbruks-universitet, Umeå, Sweden.

Krugman, S.L. and Jenkinson, J.L. (1974): Pinus. In Seeds of Woody Plants in the United States. Agric. Handbook 450, Forest Service, USDA, Washington D.C.

Laurie, M.V. (1974): Tree planting practices in African Savannas. FAO For. Dev. Paper No. 19. FAO Rome.

Leadem, C. L. 1989. Stratification and quality assessment of Abies lasiocarpa seeds. Canada-British Columbia FRDA Report 095, ISSN 0835-0752, 18 p.

Muller, C., M. Bonnet-Masimbert, and E. Laroppe. 1990 Nouvelles vo ies dans le traitement des graines dormantes de certains feuillus: hêtre, frêne, merisier. Rev. For. Fr. 42(3):329-345

Muller, C. and M. Bonnet-Masimbert. 1989. Breaking dormancy before storage: a great improvement to processing of beechnuts. Seed Sci. Technol. 17: 15-26.

Pattanath, P.G. (1982): Personal communication.

Seeber, G. and Agpaoa, A. (1976): Forest Tree Seeds. In Manual of Reforestation and Erosion Control for the Philippines, 473–535. German Agency for Technical Co-operation, Eschborn

Suszka, B., C. Muller, and M. Bonnet-Masimbert. 1996. Seeds of forest broad- leaves. From harvest to sowing. Translated by A. Gordon. Institute National de la Recherche Agronomique, Paris. 297 p.

Valencia, A.R. (1973): Germination of Moluccan Sav (Albizia falcata) seeds soaked in hot water. Occ. Pap. Bur. of For., Philippines, No. 50.

Wunder, W.G. (1966): The handling of seed in Sudan forestry. Pamphlet No. 19, Sudan Forests Dept. and UNDP Forestry Research and Education Project. Forest Res. Inst., Soba, Khartoum.

5

Seed Testing

Seed testing

No matter how good processed seed may look, the actual value is the number of seedlings it will produce. Testing of seeds is therefore imperative to determine and identify the changes that have occurred from the time of collection until the seeds are sold or sown at one time. The critical step in evaluating a seed lot is the drawing of representative sample. Place all the test samples in a bucket, mix them thoroughly and subdivide to obtain sample size. Improvements in seed processing can only be obtained with quality control. These evaluations should be made in the processing plant and at a seed testing laboratory. The National Tree Seed Laboratories offers a free service to evaluate processing machinery. You need only collect a small sample of seed after it has been processed by each machine and send it to the laboratory. Be sure all the seed comes from the same lot so all samples are related. Each machine must be adjusted for efficient operation, and proper adjustment requires monitoring of the operation.

Following the processing, an evaluation should be made of the moisture content, particularly if the seed will be placed in storage immediately. Although samples can be sent to a seed laboratory, an electronic moisture meter at the processing plant will save time, improve accuracy and provide an opportunity to take immediate action. Laboratory tests are essential for identification of possible changes during storage, identification of problem lots and providing needed data for computing sowing rates. The National Tree Seed Laboratories also provides a free service for solving seed processing problems. The seed laboratory will attempt to solve your problem on its laboratory machines and provide a report on the results.

The most critical step in evaluating a seed lot is the drawing of a representative sample. If drums are filled in consecutive order during processing, a 1,000-pound seed lot can be quite variable. Most likely, the first drum will not relate to the last drum in test results. Also, unless the whole 1,000 pounds is to be sold or sown at one time, the test results may not truly apply to the portion to be sold or sown and the samples drawn accordingly. The most complete method is to take three probes, from top to bottom, of each container with a seed trier. Place all probe samples in a bucket, mix thoroughly and subdivide to obtain sample size. For very small lots (10 pounds or less) of improved seed, it is better to pour the seed into a conical pile and subdivide them with a stick or ruler into quarters. if one quarter is still too large, repeat the process with that portion.

Seed sizing

The real benefits of seed sizing are more uniform germination in the nursery and a more uniform seedling density in the seedbed. Both of these qualities are very important in the nursery to increase the seedling-to-seed ratio. A study of sizing slash pine showed that gravity separation did not significantly add to seedbed uniformity but screen sizing did (Belcher, et al 1984). Seedling height, root collar diameter and seedling weight were all related to seed size. Using discretion in sizing seed is so dogmatic that sized portions are too small to adequately handle. A reasonable recommendation is not to establish separate sizes for portions of lots which constitute less than 10 percent of the total. Portions that are small should be thoroughly mixed with the next size. Sizing should not be considered with lots so uniform in size that less than 20 percent of the total falls into any one size. Sizing seed has been criticized on the basis that it may eliminate some genotypes (Silen and Osterhaus 1978). Actually, no genotypes are lost unless one or more seed sizes are discarded. In fact, sizing may preserve slower germinating genotypes (Wasser, 1979). State nurseries serving many landowners may need to consider genetic diversity when seedlings are grown from sized seed. Some landowners may desire mixed seedlings to produce a more heterogeneous stand. These seedlings could withstand a greater variety of environmental hazards.

Table 1. Average seed sizes of some tree species

Scientific name	**Seeds per gram**		**Scientific name**	**Seeds per gram**	
	Average	**Range**		**Average**	**Range**
Gymnosperms			**Angiosperms**		
Abies amabelis	25	18-36	*Acer macrophyllum*	7	6-8
A. grandis	50	26-63	*Alnus rubra*	1468	844-2396
Juniperous scopudorum	60	39-93	*Betula paperfera*	3040	1344-9083
Larix luricini	701	463-926	*Fraxinus lavifolia*	18	13-21
L. lyallii	313	231-359	*Populus balsamifera*	3766	3583-3949
L. occidentalis	302	216-434	*P. tremuloides*	8353	5984-10707
Picea engelmannii	300	152-709	*Prunus emarginata*	15	9-19

P. glauca	405	298-884	*Quercus garryana*	0.19	0.17-0.22
P. stichensis	465	341-881	*Salix amyglaloides*	5720	4954- 6486
Pinus banksiana	209	156-551	*S. babbilionica*	5500	4874-6126
P. contorta	263	225-300	*S. luccida*	25000	23550-26450
P. ponderosa	25	15-51			
P. albicaulis	6	5-7			
Psedosuga menziesii	85	63-117			
Taxus brevifolia	34	32-36			
Thuja plicanta	915	447-1307			
T. heterophylla	655	416-1119			
T. merinsiana	251	132-458			

Sources: Stein *et al.* (1986); Wyckoff and Zasada (1998); Zasada and Strong (1998)

Determining number of seeds per unit weight

The number of seeds per unit weight is determined from the pure seed fraction of purity test. If purity test is not made, the seed can be blown clean and remaining debris removed by hand. This seed lot will; however, contain both filled and empty seeds. The results are determined by counting five replicates of 100 seeds per unit. Weigh each unit of seeds and record the figure. Now get the average seed weight per unit. Subtract the weight of heaviest unit from that of lightest unit recorded for five replicates. Note that if the difference is greater than 10 percent of the average repeat the process (Table 2).

Table 2. Determining number of seeds per unit weight

Sample	Weight (g)
1	5.30
2	5.31
3	5.42
4	5.44
5	5.58
Average	**5.41**

Average x 10 percent = 0.54

Heaviest – lightest = 5.58-5.30 = 0.28

If 0.28 had been greater than 0.54, a re-test would be required. If results are acceptable, double the 500- seed total to get 1000- seed weight and then compute the number of seeds per pound by the following formula:

$$\text{Seeds per pound} = \frac{453,600}{1000 \text{ - seed weight (g)}}$$

Determining purity

Purity is a measure of cleanliness. Another view point is that it indicates how well the seeds were processed. It is obtained by separating trash from given sample of the seed lot. To perform a purity test a given sample is weighed, the trash and impurities are separated and weighed. If the weight of the original sample and the total weight of the components differ by more than 1 percent, draw another sample. Purity is computed as:

$$\text{Percent purity} = \frac{\text{Weight of clean seeds}}{\text{Weight of total sample}} \times 100$$

A purity test is important when sowing seed by weight or number of particles because trash is excluded from germination tests. Further, because purity is based on weight, any determination of good or bad cleaning must refer to the type of impurity. Seed wings are light and therefore a lot of wings would have to be present to reduce the purity to 90 percent, while resin balls are heavy and are hardly noticeable at 90 percent purity (Fig 2).

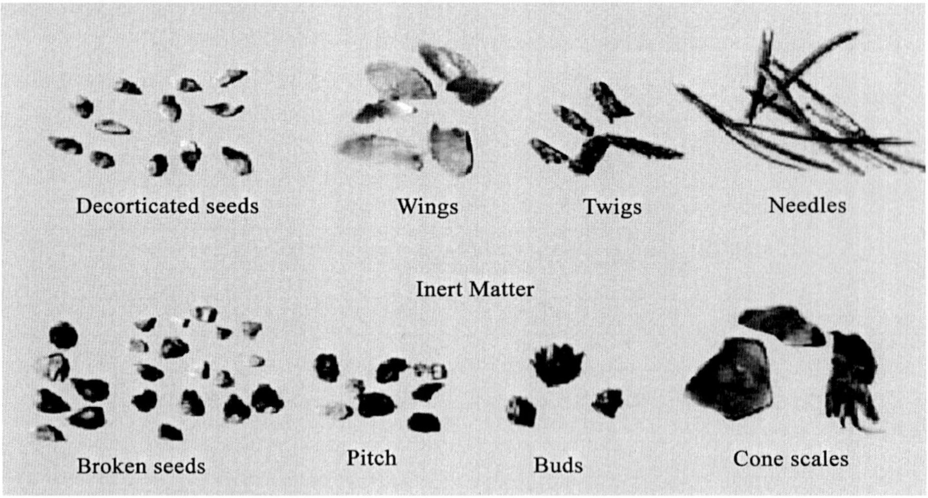

Fig. 1. Common impurities in seed samples.

Seed quality and vigor

The loss (21%) of trees in forest nurseries is caused by failure of seed to germinate. This loss results from lack of recognition of the interaction between seed vigor and environmental stress. The potential of a seed to develop into an independent seedling is referred to as seed quality, which is usually, assessed using germination and vigour tests. Vigour tests attempt to predict performance under a variety of conditions. They are potentially a more sensitive indicator of seed performance because vigour declines more rapidly than viability. Decreasing seed vigor is reflected in lower germination. The more vigorous the seed, the shorter the number of days to reach 90 percent of the total germination. As yet, no single test has been found to adequately quantify seed vigour, but most attempts have been based on characteristics that distinguish vigorous from non-vigorous seeds. These characteristics include:

- Seeds that germinate rapidly are better able to compete for available water, light, and nutrients.
- All seeds germinate well under optimum temperatures, but vigorous seeds germinate well under a wide range of temperatures.
- Respiration may vary, depending on the seed's moisture content or stage of germination, but higher than normal rates signal impaired physiological activity.
- Seeds are incubated under very low temperatures, or under very high temperature and humidity conditions. Vigorous seeds germinate better, and are more resistant to attack by fungi or moulds.

The principal behind testing of seed vigor is that seeds generally die progressively and not all at once. This means that a given seed lot contains dead, weak and dying and as well as sound seeds. While germination test provides a standard of living and the dead, seed vigor provides a measure of calculating weak and dying seeds from a living portion (Belcher, 1978). Assuming that the same portion is dying that has already died (Table 3).

$$\text{Weak and dying} = \text{germination \%} \times \text{(percent dead seeds)}$$

Thus seed lot with 75 percent germination contains 25 percent dead seed and further 25 percent of living seeds are weak and dying. The weak and dying seed would be 19 percent (0.75 x 0 .25). So the potential of that lot would be 56 percent (75-19).

Table 3. Proforma for purity and viability test

Test No	Date	Purity (%)	No. of pure seeds per kg	No. of viable seeds per kg	Empty Seeds (%)	Conversion Factor	Re-marks

Moisture content

Accurate determination of moisture content is required for both seed storage and seed treatment. The first point to appreciate is that, even when the seed is fully imbibed and equilibrated, different parts of the seed will have different moisture contents. It is therefore important to determine if the recommended moisture content is for the embryo, the whole seed or the whole fruit. Generally, the covering layer around the embryo has lower moisture content than the rest of the seed and so recommendations for whole fruit moisture content will be lower than those for the seed or the embryo.

Methods of determining moisture content of seeds have been classified by Justice (1972) into:

a) Basic methods in which the moisture is driven out of the seeds by heat and measured by the loss of weight of the original material, or the weight or volume of the condensed moisture.

b) Practical methods designed for rapid routine work and standardized against one or more of the basic methods.

Probably all the moisture cannot be driven out of seeds without driving out small amounts of other volatile constituents or causing chemical changes in the material which would result in weight changes. In applying any method, therefore, it is necessary to adhere closely to the prescribed procedure in order that the results of all tests made by that method would be comparable.

Until recently ISTA prescribed three possible procedures:

1. Drying in an oven for 17 hours at 103°C
2. Drying in an oven for one to four hours at 130°C
3. Toluene distillation.

Method (2) is applicable only to certain agricultural seeds and method (3) previously used for *Abies, Cedrus, Fagus, Picea, Pinus* and Tsuga has now been eliminated (ISTA 1981). This leaves only method (1) - the "Low constant temperature oven method" which is applicable to forest tree seeds.

The test should be made on two samples of about 5 g each, drawn from the working sample including impurities and not on pure seeds. Large seeds should be ground, broken or cut into small fragments to facilitate drying. A rule of thumb is to break any seed that averages over 10 mm in diameter or length (Bonner 1981). The samples should be weighed and placed in metal containers that are well-spaced to facilitate air circulation within an oven which is maintained at a temperature of 103° ± 2°C for 17 ± 1 hours. At the end of that period the seed should be placed in a desiccator to cool for 30 – 45 minutes and then reweighed. The relative humidity in the laboratory where the final weighing is done should be less than 70%, to avoid rapid re-absorption of moisture. The difference in MC of the two samples should not exceed a stated tolerance percentage. If it does, a further pair of samples should be tested; otherwise the mean of the two samples is the final result. The tolerance earlier prescribed by ISTA for all species was 0.2% but, as pointed out by Gordon (1979) and Bonner (1981), a single tolerance figure is not applicable to all species. The tolerance limits for moisture tests in tree seeds as approved by ISTA (1983) are given in Table 4.

Table 4. Tolerance limits for moisture tests in tree seeds.

Sample Condition	**Tolerance %**
Small seeds, moisture <12%, e.g. Picea, Alnus	0.3
Large seeds, moisture <12%, e.g. Carya	0.4
Small seeds, moisture >12%	0.5
Large seeds, moisture 12 to 25%	0.8
Large Seeds, moisture > 25%, e.g. Quercus	2.5

The calculation of moisture content should be made on a wet weight or fresh weight basis.

$$\text{Moisture Content (\%)} = \frac{\text{Original weight}}{\text{Original weight}} \times 100$$

Although wet weight basis is prescribed by ISTA and is becoming increasingly the standard form for expressing moisture content, it is not yet universal. To avoid any doubt, the method of calculating moisture content should be stated explicitly on any certificate or statement of results.

As explained by Gordon and Rowe (1982); provided that the initial fresh weight of a seed lot is measured and the initial moisture content (wet weight basis) calculated by oven-drying a sample, any new MC reached as a result of drying (or wetting) can be calculated directly from the new weight of the seed lot; there is no need for further oven-drying of samples at the new MC. The desired weight of the seed lot to be achieved through drying (or wetting) can be calculated by multiplying its initial weight by the initial dry matter percentage and dividing by the desired dry matter percentage (Table 5).

Table 5. Example for calculation of seed MC (%)

1. If initial wet weight of a seed lot = 50 kg and the MC (wet weight basis), determined by oven-drying a sample, is 25%, the oven-dry weight = 75% of wet weight = 37.5 kg.

2. If a period of drying reduces the wet weight to 46.5 kg, the new MC

$$\text{Wet weight basis} = \frac{(46.5 - 37.5)}{46.5} = 19.4\%$$

3. If it is desired to reduce the MC (wet weight basis) to 10%, then desired oven-dry weight will be 90% of new wet weight and the seed lot must be further dried until its wet weight is:

$$\text{Wet weight} = \frac{(50 - 75)}{90} = 41.67\%$$

Germination Testing

Sample for Germination Testing: Transfer Envelope

From Seed Store **To** **Testing Laboratory**

Species: ....

Official Identity No. ....

Sample No. .... of .... Weighing .... gm and representing .... kg of seed in .... storage containers

Date of sampling ....

Sampled by ....

Table 7. Sample Seed Testing Ledger Sheet

Test No	Species	Ident. No	Date Sample Rec.	Tests to be Performed and Results						No. Germ. (viable) Seeds/ kg	Remarks
				M. C.	Purity	1000 Pure Seed Weight	Germination	Viability			
								TZ	EET		
A1											
A2											
A3											
A4 etc.											
B1											
B2											

*** letter changes at start of new seed testing year**

*** including year of production, seed stand identification**

Source: Forest Research Station, Alice Holt, UK.

Germination value

The concept of Germination Value, as defined by Czabator (1962), aims to combine in a single figure an expression of total germination at the end of the test period with an expression of germination energy or speed of germination. Total germination is expressed as (final) Mean Daily Germination (MDG), calculated as the cumulative percentage of full seed germination at the end of the test, divided by the number of days from sowing to the end of the test. Speed of germination is expressed as Peak Value, which is the maximum mean daily germination (cumulative percentage of full seed germination divided by number of days elapsed since sowing date) reached at any time during the period of the test. Germination Value (GV) can then be calculated from the formula.

$$GV = \text{(final) MDG} \times PV$$

Djavanshir and Pourbeik (1976) proposed an alternative method for calculating Germination Value. The formula they used is:

$$GV = (\sum DGS / N) \times \frac{GP}{10}$$

where,

GV	=	Germination value
GP	=	Germination percent at the end of the test
DGS	=	Daily germination speed, obtained by dividing the cumulative germination percent by the number of days since sowing
∑DGS	=	The total obtained by adding every DGS figure obtained from the daily counts
N	=	The number of daily counts, starting from the date of first germination

Germination energy

Germination Energy has been defined as the number of seeds in a given sample which germinate within a given period e.g. in 7 or 14 days, under optimum or stated conditions. or The percent, by number of seeds in a given sample which germinate up to the time of peak germination. The interest in germinative energy is based on a theory that only those seeds which germinate rapidly and vigorously under the favourable conditions of the laboratory are likely to be capable of producing vigorous seedlings in field conditions, where weak or delayed germination is often fatal (Aldhous, 1972). The method of comparing germination energy of different seed lots is to record “Rate of Germination” i.e. the number of days required to attain 50% of germination capacity (Allen, 1958). The shorter the period, the greater the germination energy. Yet another method is to evaluate the stage of development of germinated seeds and classify them into a number of development or vigour classes. For example Wang (1976) used seven classes for germinated normal seeds of Picea glauca, in addition to ungerminated and abnormally germinated seeds; they ranged from seedlings with healthy root, fully developed hypocotyl and seedcoat completely shed to seeds with seedcoat burst open but as yet no radicle emergence.

Germination testing in the nursery

A suitable method for testing germination in the nursery has been recommended by Paul (1972) (Table 8):

- Take 400 pure seed and divide them into 4 sub-samples each of 100 seeds.
- Take 4 wooden or plastic boxes of dimensions 30 × 30 cm with a depth of about 10 cm and fill them slightly overfull with sand, which has been passed through a Mesh No. 12 (12/64" or 4.76 mm) but retained on a Mesh No. 8 (Size 8/64" or 3.18 mm).
- Wet the sand by applying 0.5 litres of water to each box.
- Level the sand across the top of each box and make drills of 6 mm depth at 2.5 cm intervals.
- Sow the seed at prescribed intervals and gently press them in the drill.
- Cover the seeds with sand and apply water with a fine mist spray.
- Cover with transparent polythene sheeting of 0.2 mm thickness mounted on the upper side of a square tight-fitting wooden frame of 5 cm thickness. Within 24 hours condensation of moisture will appear on the inside of the polythene cover.
- If moisture disappears at any time during the ensuing 7 days then give a light mist spray and close lid once more.
- Germination will usually begin by the 7th day and the cover can be removed. A seed is recorded as having germinated when it has reached a height of 1 cm with seed coat enclosing the cotyledons. Record all germination from 7th to 28th day separately for each of the four boxes.
- Prick out seedlings as soon as they are recorded and remove any diseased ones as they may infect others.

Table 8. Test made on 4 × 100 seed replicates from the pure seed component of the purity test.

Replicate No.	**1**	**2**	**3**	**4**	**Total**	**Mean**
No. germinated on completion of test	79	85	76	88	328	82
Sound seeds on cutting test	4	3	6	3	16	4

Germination %	=	82%
Viability %	=	82 + 4 = 86%

Viable seeds per unit weight

While use of the germination percent will indicate the number of germinable seeds, the combination of the viability percent and weight of pure seed will give a figure for the number of viable seeds expected per unit weight of pure seed. Incorporation of a factor for purity percent will express the numbers in terms of the number of viable or germinable seeds per unit weight of "impure" seed.

Table 9. Determination of purity percent.

Particulars	Pure Seed	
	per g	per kg
No. of viable seeds	26.6 × 86 ÷ 100 = 22.9	22,900
No. of germinable seeds	26.6 × 82 ÷ 100 = 21.8	21,800
	Impure Seed	
	per g	per kg
No. of viable seeds	22.9 × 91 ÷ 100 = 20.8	20,800
No. of germinable seeds	21.8 × 91 ÷ 100 = 19.8	19,800

For very small-seeded species the number of germinated seeds per unit weight of impure seed is determined directly by test (Table 9). Figures for numbers of pure seeds per unit weight are not obtainable for this type of seed. Although usually expressed as "viable seeds per g", it should be noted that a cutting test is also impracticable for these small seeds, so strictly speaking the figures refer to germinable seeds.

Inspection of the pattern of germination (Annexure 7) suggests that rejection of all seeds germinating after peak germination would result in the rejection of an excessive proportion (60 %) of the potentially germinable seeds, while acceptance of all germinable seeds would unduly prolong the period of test and probably result in the inclusion of some seedlings of very poor vigour. A sensible rule of thumb applicable to the type of germination pattern in this example would be to define the energy period as lasting until daily germination falls to less than 25 % of peak (Table 10).

Table 10. Calculation of germination value, by the methods of Czabator (1962) and Djavanshir and Pourbeik (1976)

Days since sowing	Daily Germination Percent	Cumulative Germination Percent	Daily Germination Speed (or Mean Germination) (Col. 3 ÷ Col. 1)	Σ DGS	No. of counts	Σ DGS/N (Col.5 ÷ Col.6)
1	2	3	4	5	6	7
8	7.25	7.25	0.91	0.91	1	0.91
9	7.75	15.00	1.67	2.58	2	1.29
10	11.00	26.00	2.60	5.18	3	1.73
11	9.00	35.00	3.18	8.36	4	2.09

12	5.75	40.75	3.40	11.76	5	2.35
13	4.50	45.25	3.48	15.24	6	2.54
14	3.25	48.50	3.46	18.70	7	2.67
15	2.50	51.00	3.40	22.10	8	2.76
16	3.00	54.00	3.38	25.48	9	2.83
17	1.25	55.25	3.25	28.73	10	2.87
18	2.00	57.25	3.18	31.91	11	2.90
19	0.75	58.00	3.05	34.96	12	2.91
20	1.25	59.25	2.96	37.92	13	2.92
21	0.50	59.75	2.85	40.77	14	2.91
22	1.25	61.00	2.77	43.54	15	2.90
23	1.00	62.00	2.70	46.24	16	2.89
24	0.75	62.75	2.61	48.85	17	2.87
25	0.75	63.50	2.54	51.39	18	2.86
26	0.00	63.50	2.44	53.83	19	2.83
27	0.00	63.50	2.35	56.18	20	2.81
28	0.50	64.00	2.29	58.47	21	2.78

1. Czabator method

   Germination value = Final DSG × Peak Value DGS = 2.29×3.48 = 7.97.

2. Djavanshir and Pourbeik method

   Germination value = (Final ∑ DGS (N) × (Final Cumulative Germination %/10) = 2.78 × 6.4 = 17.79.

Field germination in an operational nursery will often differ from test germination. It may be considerably lower than that in the ideal conditions of a laboratory test and somewhat lower than that in a research nursery. It should differ very little from a test carried out in the same nursery in advance of the main sowings (Table 11).

Table 11. Difference between laboratory and nursery germination (Wunder, 1966)

Species	**Laboratory germination % in days**		**Nursery germination % in days**		**Pretreatment**
Cedrela odorata	100	3	85	18	
Prosopis chilensis	100	15	79	38	2 minutes in conc. H_2SO_4
Acacia raddiana	100	3	30	4	60 minutes in conc. H_2SO_4

Seed vigor

After you examine the presented facts on a germination report, evaluate the comparative value of lots. If more than one lot exists for each source, use the lot that will survive the shortest time in storage. In other cases, selection may have to be made on the intended use of the seed. Will it be used for direct seeding, bare-root seeding or container stock?

The simplest evaluation embraces the concept that seeds die progressively and not all at once. Therefore, a given seed lot contains dead, weak and dying seed & sound seed. The germination test provides a measure of the living and the dead; therefore, we must calculate the weak and dying from the living portion (Belcher, 1978). Assume that the same portion is dying that has already died. Use this formula:

weak and dying = germination x (percent dead seed)

Thus, a seed lot with 75-percent germination contains 25 percent dead seed and, further 25 percent of the living seed are weak and dying. The weak and dying seed would be 19 percent (.75 x .25). So the potential of that lot would be 56 percent (75 - 19) (item F on figure 5-11). The greatest loss (21 percent) of trees in forest nurseries is caused by failure of the seed to germinate (Rowan, 1970). This loss results from the lack of recognition of the interaction between seed vigor and environmental stress. Decreasing seed vigor is reflected in lower germination. In a seedbed situation, laboratory germination rates will seldom be realized.

A second evaluation can be made by plotting the germination data over time. Note on the germination curve in figure 5-9 the number of days to reach the "shoulder" or break in the curve. To calculate the number of days rather than use a graph, multiply the total germination by 90 percent; then calculate the number of days to reach that point. Most seedlings produced after this point in the laboratory will not result in a tree in the nursery. The more vigorous the seed the shorter the number of days to reach 90 percent of the total. Tests producing a slow-rising germination curve will be subjected to longer field conditions during germination, which will result in lower field germination. Some nursery managers prefer to use the time required to reach 50 percent germination rather than 90 percent.

A third method to measure seed vigor is to use Czabator's germination value (Czabator, 1962). The value is a combination of germination speed quantity with emphasis on speed. Germination should be of prime importance to nursery managers. If germination starts slowly, the seed will become prey to birds, rodents, fungal organisms and any adverse environment. The germination value (GV) is calculated by the formula:

GV = PV x MDG

GV = PV x mean daily germination

The peak value (PV) is obtained by dividing the germination rate by the number of days at that count. This average will increase at each count to some peak value and then decrease- The mean daily germination (MDG) is the average value on a given day, usually the last day of the test. When you compare seed lots, use the same final day. The faster the seed germinate, the shorter time required between counts to estimate the true peak value. Germination values per se are meaningless, but when two lots are compared or when two tests on the same lot are compared, the more active or vigorous lots can be identified by the higher value.

Tests for viability

Pollen viability tests

The extent to which any applied pollination program is successful depends principally on the viability of the pollen. Therefore, viability testing is a core step of any pollen application program. Laboratory viability tests are available to test potential fertility in most conifer species, including western hemlock. The procedures for hemlock are adopted primarily from those developed for Douglas-fir, which are summarized in Webber and Bonnet-Masimbert (1993) and Webber and Painter (1996). The procedures we developed can estimate pollen viability, relative vigour (rate of pollen tube growth), and potential fertility. These tests were developed primarily to estimate the effects of storage on pollen fertility. However, they are also useful for estimating potential fertility of pollen at all stages of handling (e.g., pollen collection and extraction), as well as estimating the yearly variation in pollen viability attributed to environmental effects.

Another important application of viability tests is in formulating specific pollen mixes for improving the genetic worth of production seed lots. Paternal success of individual lots within the mix is affected by its viability. If any particular pollen lot has a significantly lower fertility potential, then the contribution from that lot will be less or not realized at all. Previously, we recommended formulations of pollen mixes with no fewer than 15–20 lots. In this way, probability would dictate whether a low viability pollen lot is in competition with a higher viability lot. More recently, Stoehr *et al.* (1999) showed that formulating pollen poly-mixes on the basis of viability rather than of volume is an effective way to balance paternal contribution and therefore improve effective population size (Ne). Under open pollination conditions, where competition from high viability pollen occurs, the estimates of potential parental contribution from pollen lots with a low viability may not be realized.

There are many types of laboratory assays to indicate pollen viability but three are most useful for the conifers we have tested. These are:

i. Respiration: a measure of oxygen uptake under controlled conditions.
ii. Conductivity: a measure of the conductivity of an aqueous pollen leachate, and
iii. Germination: a measure of pollen grain growth under controlled conditions.

The following five subsections contain a discussion on pollen preconditioning, which is a necessary first step for testing most conifer pollen lots, a general discussion of each of the three assays, and a final section on the correlation of assay response to field fertility.

Pollen preconditioning

When pollen is taken from storage it is in a dormant, dehydrated state, and, before metabolic activity is restored, uptake of water is essential. Imbibition of water depends to a large extent on the osmotic status of the pollen grain and its surrounding environment. Under natural conditions, conifer pollen is shed in a hydrated state, and further water uptake to complete germination and tube growth readily takes place within the micropyle. The same is true for most conifer pollen being tested for viability. Pre-hydration just prior to the assay improves both the assay response and its relationship to field fertility. The effect of pre-hydration on assay response for western hemlock pollen is shown for each of the three assays described below. For respiration and germination procedures, pre-hydration did not improve assay response or the relationship to field fertility.

Conductivity

Conductivity is a direct measure of pollen membrane stability.When pollen is dehydrated, pollen membranes lose their structural integrity and viability. The extent of this effect depends on the species and the level of moisture reduction. As pollen moisture content is reduced, the membranes become more porous, resulting in reduced membrane activity and an increase in pollen cellular content that can be leached. Since this leachate carries an electrical charge, simple conductivity measurements of the leachate provide a direct estimate of membrane damage and reductionin viability. The procedure is relatively simple and the assay can be completed in less than hours. However, as for all laboratory assays, more reliable estimates of potential fertility can be made if conductivity is assessed with either germination or respiration results.

Germination

Pollen grains of most conifer species will germinate and grow a pollen tube when cultured in a suitable medium. Of all the conifer species, western hemlock forms the longest tubes both under natural conditions and in culture. Although germination response to laboratory and field conditions may be different, the techniques we have developed for assessing laboratory response are still a good measure of a pollen lot's potential fertility. Most conifer pollen grains can readily germinate in aqueous solutions with little or no added nutrition. However, in water alone germination is often incomplete. Tube lengths are shorter and in many cases pollen grains will burst if the osmotic potential of the pollen grain and the solution are considerably different. Mature pollen grains normally carry sufficient food reserves (free sugars, starch, lipids, and protein) to enable them to be independent identities from the time of pollen shedding through germination and early tube growth. In general, conifer pollen can be cultured on relatively simple media. Several factors affect pollen response in culture, among which hydration state and medium composition are the most important.

Seed viability tests

All nursery workers should realize that most seeds are at their maximum viability at the time of collection. As the seeds age their vigor declines. However, if the seeds have been properly handled a viability may be maintained for years. Reports have identified 18-year-old loblolly pine seeds with 90-percent germination (Belcher and Karrfalt 1976). Estimating the viability of a seed lot by actually germinating a sample of it is often the method most relevant to practical forestry. But the tests take several weeks to complete and for some species pretreatment may take some additional time. For this reason much research has been conducted to find other methods by which seed viability can be estimated accurately but much more rapidly than by germination testing. The following account of these methods closely follows that of Turnbull (1975).

The objects of quick viability tests are:

- To determine quickly the viability of seeds which normally germinate slowly or show dormancy under the normal germination methods.
- To determine the viability of samples which at the end of the germination test reveal a high percentage of fresh ungerminated or hard seeds.

  The ISTA has accepted five methods, the cutting test, the tetrazolium test, the hydrogen peroxide test, the embryo excision test and as official methods for testing the seed viability. The X-ray test is; however, considered as a valid alternative to the cutting test for the detection of empty and insect-damaged seeds.

Tetrazolium test

The normal practice is to soak the seeds in water for about 20 hours followed by cutting or puncturing the seed coat and finally immersing the seeds in 1% aqueous solution of tetrazolium (TZ) for 48 hours (dark) to facilitate entry of the chemical. This chemical is reduced to a red precipitate by the action of enzymes. The net result is that where intact enzymes are present, the seed is stained red. The process can be greatly speeded up by cutting through the seed at a distance of one third from the micropyle and placing it in a Vitascope vacuum machine for half hour. The uniformity and intensity of the stain are related to seed vigor. When this test is performed by an experienced, skilled technician, the estimate of seed vigor is closely correlated with that obtained from the standard germination test. The advantage of this test is that it is relatively rapid, as only three days are required to complete an evaluation.

Although this method gives satisfactory results, the interpretation of results requires more experience in the operator than the method of seed immersion followed by excision of the stained embryo (Knudsen, 1982). The test is done on 4 replicates of 100 seeds each (ISTA 1976). Justice (1972) states that while the tetrazolium procedure is good in principle, its practical use in routine testing is limited by many problems, including:

- Difficulty in staining of some seeds.
- Necessity of cutting or dissecting seeds to permit observation of stained parts.
- Poor agreement with results of germination tests in some cases, especially for seed of low germination capacity.
- Lack of uniform interpretation of staining and difficulty in interpreting the significance of different degrees of staining.
- Increase in man-hours required to test 400 seeds compared to regular germination tests.

Hydrogen peroxide

This test has been used by seed testing laboratories as one of the quickest measures of seed viability. The seeds are soaked overnight in 1% H_2O_2. The seed coat is then cut open to expose the radicle tip and the seeds put back into 1% H_2O_2 in the dark at alternating temperatures (20° and 30°C) for several days. Counting and refreshment of H_2O_2 is done after 3 or 4 days and at the end of a week, the growth of the radicle is measured and the viability of the seed estimated. Radicle growth of 5 mm or more is scored “evident”, 0-5 mm “slight” and no growth means a nonviable or empty seed (Danielson, 1972) (Fig 6). The advantages of this test are:

1. It is an actual measure of growth.
2. It is relatively rapid and simple to perform than excised embryo and easier to interpret.
3. It requires less manipulation than either the tetrazolium test or the excised embryo and is, therefore, less expensive.

The disadvantages are:

1. It requires skilled personnel and is more expensive than other standard tests.
2. It does not identify anomalous germination.

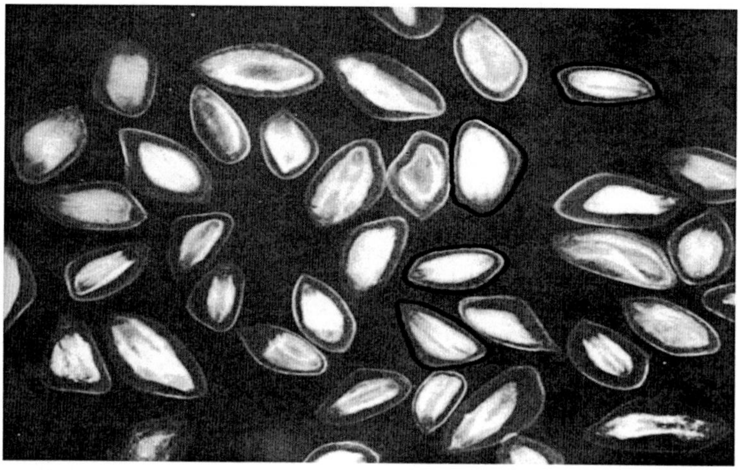

Fig. 1. Seeds treated with hydrogen peroxide.

Excised embryo test

Research has shown that, when embryos are removed from seeds, they will germinate more rapidly than they do in intact seeds. Accordingly, this test involves removing the embryos after soaking seeds in water for 1-4 days and then incubating the embryos under carefully controlled conditions for a period of from eight to ten days. The excised embryos are then placed on moist filter paper or blotter discs in petri dishes which are placed under light at a constant temperature of 20°C. The condition of the embryos is examined daily. Depending upon the species and seed lot differences, the tests can be terminated after a maximum of 14 days, or as soon as distinct differentiation between viable and non-viable embryos can be made. The advantage of this test is that it is relatively rapid and employs a measure of actual growth to estimate seed viability. The excised embryo test is similar to germination tests in that it measures the quality of the seed by their actual germination. In addition it allows some measure of the embryo dormancy to be made, by counting those seeds which, have grown slightly, remained firm and have maintained their colour during the test period. The disadvantage is that the success of this test requires considerable skill and experience in the operator and the ISTA rules restrict it to only a few species.

X-ray radiographic test

X-ray radiographic technique described by Simak and Gustafsson (1953) is a diagnostic method of tree seed analysis. This method which uses various contrast or radiopaque agents (Simak 1957; Kamra 1963 a, 1963 b) to determine the mechanical damage and abnormally developed internal seed structures besides permitting the detection of empty seeds, measurement of the thickness of the seedcoat and assessment of the seed viability when combined with a contrast agent. Evaluation of germination potential is not made; rather the test reports only the number of seeds in each category.

Radiographs have the advantage over cutting tests by providing permanent file copies, which are more accurate in detail. In addition, a radiograph can be made in about 1 minute and evaluated within 2 or 3 minutes, which is much faster than cutting tests and does not destroy the seed.The X-ray contrast method is based on the principle of semi-permeability. When seeds are treated with a contrast agent, for example aqueous BaCl2 or vaporous CHC13, their living tissues are able to prevent its entry due to their semi-permeability, but the dead tissues become impregnated. The impregnated tissues absorb X-radiation more intensively than the unimpregnated ones and thus appear lighter on the film (Kamra, 1964). There are now possibilities of using non-toxic water, instead of toxic BaCl2 or CHC13, as a contrast agent for testing seed viability (Simak, 1982)

The development of soft X-ray equipment has greatly simplified the operation (Belcher 1973). Complicated photographic equipment is not necessary and pictures can be made with polaroid film which provides clear and detailed radiographs within 30 seconds (Edwards, 1973). Another technique - stereo-radiography; as a supplement to the X-ray contrast method, has been developed by Kamra, Meyer and Wegelius (1973). The chief advantage of stereo-radiography is that it is possible for the observer to have a three-dimensional view of the object from a pair of radiographs. In this way, the exact topographical location of the contrast agent in the seed can be reliably determined.

Table 12. Germinability (%) of freshly collected undamaged seeds belonging to different DCs, selected by radiography (Temperature 23°C constant, light 1000 lux 8 hours/day).

Species	DC							
	I A	II A	III A	IV A	II P	II B	III B	IV B
Pinus sylvestris	0	50	88	99	0	5	43	68
Picea abies	0	36	82	97	0	15	71	92

The X-ray method is very useful and is likely to play an increasing role in seed testing. Earlier models of X-ray machines were expensive, but recent models, particularly from Japan are much cheaper and now cost less than a cabinet germinator. Improvements in photographic films and paper have speeded up the process and simplified the interpretation, so that technicians can be trained easily to produce consistent results (Table 12). ISTA has accepted the method as a valid alternative to the cutting test for the detection of empty and insect damaged seeds. It also shows considerable promise for distinguishing viable and non-viable seeds among "full seeds" (Simak, 1980; Simak and Sahlén, 1981). For certain temperate conifers it has been possible to obtain good correlation between the Development Class (DC) of seeds, based on the development of both embryo and endosperm, and their germinability. The chief disadvantages of X-ray radiographs include:

1. Seed anatomy and not the seed vigor is reported.
2. Estimates of viability based upon sound, intact seeds are somewhat higher than predicted by the standard germination test.

References

Aldhous, J.R. (1972): Nursery practice. Forestry Comm. Bull. No. 43, London.

Allen, G.S. (1958) : Factors affecting the Viability and Germination Behaviour of Coniferous Seed. For. Chronicle Vol. 34, No. 3: 266–298.

Belcher, E.W. (Ed.) (1978): Small lot forest seed processing workshop, Georgia Forestry Center, Macon, Georgia, 18–20 October 1977. Eastern Tree Seed Laboratory, Macon Bonner, F.T. (1974): Seed testing. In Seeds of Woody Plants in the United States, Agriculture Handbook No. 450. For. Service, USDA, Washington D.C.

Belcher, E. W. Jr.; Leach, G. N.; Gresham, H. H. (1984). Sizing slash pine as a nursery procedure. Tree Planters' Notes. 35(2) 5-10.

Belcher, Earl W.; Karrfait, Robert P. A cooperative approach to better tree seed: Twentieth Laboratory Report, Fiscal Years 1975 and 1976, Eastern Tree Seed Laboratory. Macon, GA: U.S. Department of Agriculture, Forest Service, Southeastern Area. 1976. 37p.

Bonner, F.T. (1981): Measurement and management of tree seed moisture. Res. Paper SO-177, Southern Forest Experiment Station, USDA Forest Service.

Czabator, F.J. (1962): Germination value: An index combining speed and completeness of pine seed germination. Forest Science Vol. 8 (4), 386–396.

Djavanshir, K. and Pourbeik, H. (1976): Germination Value - a new formula. Silvae Genetica, Vol.25, 79–83

Gordon, A.G. and ROWE, D.C.F. (1982): Seed manual for ornamental trees and shrubs. For. Comm. Bull. 59, HMSO London.

ISTA (1976): International Rules for seed testing. Rules and annexes. International Seed Testing Association, Seed Sci. and Technol. 4, 3–177.

ISTA (1981): Moisture content and equipment Wkg. Group. In Report of the forest tree seed committee 1977–1980, Seed Sci. and Technol. Vol. 9 No. 1.

Justice, O.L. (1972): Essentials of seed testing. In Seed Biology Vol. 3 (Ed. T.T. Kozlowski). Academic Press New York and London, 301–370.

Kamra, S.K. (1963 a): Determination of mechanical damage on Scots pine seed with X-ray contrast method. Stud. For. Suecica 8: 1–20.

Kamra, S.K. (1963 b): Studies on a suitable contrast agent for the X-ray radiography of Norway spruce seed (Picea abies). Proc. Int. Seed Test. Ass. 28: 197–201.

Kamra, S.K. (1964): Determination of seed quality by X-rays. Adv. Frontiers of Plant Sci. 9: 119–130.

Kamra, S.K., Meyer, W.W. and Wegelius, C. (1973): Stereoradiography for increased informationaccuracy in seed quality testing. In "Seed Processing" Proc. Symposium IUFRO Wkg. Group on Seed Problems. Bergen, Vol. I, Paper 10.

Knudsen, F. (1982): Personal communication.

Moore, R.P. (1973): Tetrazolium testing practices and guides. In "Seed Processing" Proc. Symposium IUFRO Wkg. Group on Seed Problems, Bergen. Vol. I, Paper 14.

Paul, D.K. (1972): A handbook of nursery practice for Pinus caribaea var. hondurensis and other conifers in West Malaysia. Wkg. paper No. 19, FO:SF/MAL 12, UNDP/FAO Kuala Lumpur.

Rowan, S. J. (1970). Analysis of the cause and extent of losses in slash and loblolly pines in two Georgia nurseries. Tree Planters' Notes. 21(4): 20-22.

Simak, M. (1957): The X-ray contrast method for seed testing: Scots Pine -Pinus sylvestris L. Medd. f. Stat. Skogs Forsk. Instt., 47(4): 1–22.

Simak, M. (1980): X-radiography in research and testing of forest tree seeds. Sveriges Lantbruksuniversitet. Institutionen för skogsskötsel, Nr. 3.

Simak, M. (1982): Personal communication.

Simak, M. and Gustafsson, A. (1953): X-ray photography and sensitivity in forest tree species. Hereditas 39: 458–468.

Stoehr, M.U., M.C. Mullen, D.L.S. Harrison, and J.E.Webber (1999). Evaluating pollen competition in Douglas-fir using a chloroplast DNA marker. For. Gen. 6.(1):49-53.

Turnbull, J.W. (1975 d): Forest tree seed testing. In Report on FAO/DANIDA Training Course on Forest Seed Collection and Handling, Vol. 2, FAO Rome.

Wang, B.S.P. (1976): Dormancy and laboratory germination criteria of White Spruce seed. Proc. IUFRO 2nd International Symposium on Physiology of Seed Germination, Tokyo.

Wasser, R. G. (1979).Tree improvement research. In: Lantz, Clark W., comp., Proceedings, 1978 Southern nursery conference. Technical Publication SA-TP 6. Atlanta, GA: U.S. Department of Agriculture, Forest Service, Southeastern Area;; 15-25.

Webber, J.E. & R.A. Painter.(1996) Douglas-fir pollen management manual. 2nd ed. B.C.Min. For.,Res. Br., Victoria, B.C.Work. Pap.02/1996.

Webber, J.E. and M. Bonnet-Masimbert.(1993) .The response of dehydrated Douglas-Fir (Pseudotsuga menziesii) pollen to three in vitro viability assays and their relationship to actual fertility. Ann. Sci. For.903 - 22.

Wunder, W.G. (1966): The handling of seed in Sudan forestry. Pamphlet No. 19, Sudan Forests Dept. and UNDP Forestry Research and Education Project. Forest Res. Inst., Soba, Khartoum.

6

Certification of Forest Tree Seed and Plants

Need for certification

Forest restoration and reforestation experts know the effect the right seed source can have on the long-term economic and ecological success of tree planting efforts. However, unlike stock quality (such as size and health), genetic quality (seed source) cannot be observed by the consumer at the time of stock purchase. Where once the provincial government controlled the source of seed and its destination through the provincial nursery system, seed supply is now in the private sector, and the source is unknown or a matter of trust. Tree planting in general needs help, and the wrong seed source is only one of the many reasons that your planting project may not be successful. Besides, the identity of the source will be tracked throughout the chain of custody until it is presented, as a labeled, certified product to the consumer. The seed source may be from a single parent tree or preferably from a large healthy stand of trees. But if seed is bulked from many locations, the label on the resulting seedlings can only indicate the greater area. For example if a nursery bulked its seed from many counties across a specific place, they can only certify and market that crop as? specific place? not as one from a specific county that may have been a source for the seed. For this reason we will have to encourage collectors and growers to bulk only by tree seed zones to promote certification program for the context of successful tree planting.

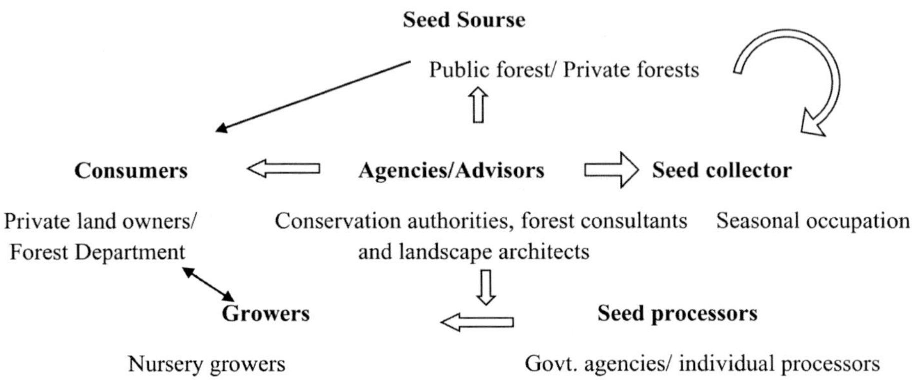

It is thus imperative to devise a program that will:

1. Certify the reforestation industry and its products.
2. Educate and help consumers to find appropriate stock.
3. To train collectors, processors and nursery growers in the documentation necessary to register their seed or stock lots so as to ensure that appropriate seed sources are used in planting programs.

Seed certification is a voluntary program operated by each State to improve seed quality and ensure genetic purity and identity in seed distribution. Tree seed certification is a guarantee issued by an official, governmental accredited authority, e.g. a seed testing station about the sourse and quality of formally documented seeds and is generally used for special valuable seeds or in connection with special requirements, e.g.:

1. Genetic quality: Seed collected from trees of proven genetic superiority, e.g. from seed orchards or superior ('plus') trees in a natural stand with controlled pollination. Certificates may state 'Certificate of Origin' or seeds may simply be referred to as 'certified tree seed' (For. Com. 1994).
2. Physiological quality: Where seed testing is carried out according to the ISTA (or AOSA) rules by special accredited seed testing laboratories, an ISTA certificate of seed quality may be issued. An ISTA seed quality certificate is hence an assurance that seeds have been tested according to the rules.
3. Health and diseases: Governments often require imported seeds to have been certified by an official authority, stating that the seeds are not infected or carrying diseases. Such a 'Phytosanitary Certificate' states that seeds have been examined and 'to the best of our knowledge' been found free of special pests and fungi.

General seed certification standards

1. Purpose of Certification: The purpose shall be to make available to the public, through certification, high quality seeds of superior plants so grown and distributed as to promote purity and identity.
2. Eligibility Requirement for Certification of seeds: Only those varieties, hybrids and species that are recommended by:
   - The Forestry, Horticultur and Agronomy Division
   - The Indian Society of Foresters
3. The following must be made available by the originator, developer, owner or Agent when eligibility for certification is requested.
   - The name of the variety. This name must be an established name if the variety has previously been marketed.
   - A statement concerning the variety.s origin and the breeding procedure used in its development.
   - A detailed description of the morphological, physiological and other characteristics of the plants and seed that distinguish it from other varieties.
   - Evidence of performance, such as purity,vigor, insect and disease resistance or other factors supporting the identity of the variety.
   - A statement delineating the geographic area or areas of adaptation of the variety.
   - Any additional restrictions on the variety specified by the breeder, with respect to geographic area of seed production, age of stand or other factors affecting genetic purity.
   - A sample of seed representative of the variety as marketed. The sample size shall be that required for a submitted sample in the current issue of the rule of Testing Seeds for the Association of Official Seed Analysts.
4. Certified Seed is t is so produced and handled as to promote satisfactory purity and identity as approved and certified by the official seed certifying agency.
5. Certified seed is tagged as
   - Certified Tree Seed (Blue Tag)
   - Selected Tree Seed (Green Tag)
   - Source . Identified Tree Seed (Yellow Tag)

6. Requirements for Certifying Agency for Training Seed Producers and Conditioners
   i. The certifying agency shall set up qualifications for seed producers and conditioners and is obligated to carry on such educational work as may be necessary to make them aware of the standards and procedures required to produce and market high quality seed.
   ii. Qualifications of acceptance of members should include: general adaptation of farm and equipment, ability of the grower, his integrity, his cooperation, and any other qualification essential to conduct a successful certified seed program.
7. Establishing the Source of Seed: Seed growers must furnish evidence of the class and source of seed used to plant each species being considered for certification. An official tag and invoice showing the amount of seed purchased is required.
8. Processors Responsibility: The Processor is solely responsible for maintaining the purity and identity of the seed at all stages of the certification process. This includes harvesting, handling, drying, storage, conditioning, bagging and labeling of the seed.
9. Seed-Borne Diseases: Every seed lot of a species for which certification is requested shall show evidence that reasonable precaution has been taken to control seedborne diseases. The seed, at the time of inspection, shall not contain beyond established tolerance of injurious seedborne diseases.
10. Field Inspection: Forest Trees meant for seed production are checked during the year for which a seed crop will be harvested. The inspections are generally made after maturity of the crop, but before harvest.
11. Analysis and test of samples of certified seed and definitions of analytic terms shall be in accordance with the rules of the Association of Official Seed Analysts.
12. Seed Conditioning: All certified seed must be conditioned. in an Approved Seed Plant.
13. The Seed Plant operator and/or an appointed representative(s) is responsible for:
    - Maintaining purity and quality of seed during all stages of handling
    - Keeping certain records
    - Pulling official samples
    - Ordering certification tags

- Attaching certification tags to the bags
- Preventing seed from being moved until official laboratory reports have been received clearing seed for certification
- Removing tags with the word Certified on bags of rejected lots of seed or retagged with an orange label (Not Certified Seed).

14. Blending: Seed lots of the same species and class may be blended and the class retained. If lots of different classes are blended, the lowest class shall be applied to the resultant blend. Such blending can only be done when authorized by the certifying agency.
15. Seed Treatment: The treatment of seed with an approved pesticide is not generally a requirement but since all seed contain seedborne diseases and are subject to damage by insects/pathogens, the Association recommends that seed normally treated, be treated for the control of seedborne diseases and insects. Note: All treated seed must be labeled according to state and federal law.
16. Substandard Seed: Any seed that meets all certification Standards, except that it germinates below the minimum ISTA standard, may be certified with tags marked of Below Standard in Germination.
17. Liability: Responsibility for any obligations, arising from the sale or shipment of seed,which has been certified, rests with the grower or subsequent handler making the sale or shipment.
18. Samples and Sampling of Seed : A representative sample of each lot of seed as it is offered for sale shall be obtained for analysis by an approved representative of the certifying agency. Those approved are:
    - An official State Seed Inspector
    - Seed plant operator or plant representative
    - Registered Seed Technologist (Board of Directors)

Guidelines for ordering tree seed

End use

It is very important to know what the plants/trees are to be used for before tree seed is ordered. Some trees provide timber, some fuel or fodder, while others may be appropriate for shelter or for fighting desertification. Some tree planters may want to establish seed or conservation stands, others provenance or progeny trials. Therefore, the purpose for which the trees are to be used should be made quite clear.

Tree species

Usually a number of tree species can fulfil the purposes in question. If both indigenous and exotic species are relevant, it may be safest to choose an indigenous species. Indigenous species have shown their ability to grow in the region and the local risk of pests and diseases is better documented. However, documentation of successful performance of exotic species may make you choose such species. If seed of an exotic is to be ordered from abroad, quarantine measures or special permissions may be necessary. It is worth investigating the results as there may be significant differences between the performance on different sites. Advice should be sought either with national or regional seed centres or with reliable seed dealers. If you already know the tree species you want to order, make sure that the name of the species is a generally accepted one. If you only know the local name, you must contact someone who knows or can look up the proper Latin or botanical name of the species. Otherwise you may receive a wrong species and this can have serious consequences.

Planting site

Through generations, trees have evolved to become better suited for the area where they live naturally. Some species have evolved in the tropics and can grow well only there, while other species grow well in other climates. This means that trees develop differently in different climates and on different planting sites, therefore it is important to know where the plants/trees are to be grown. Some tree species have a wide natural distribution and many of these have developed provenances, which are groups particularly suited for the region where they grow naturally. Growth conditions relate to temperature, rainfall, and light (day length), but they also cover soil characteristics, though these are of less importance than climatic ones. Therefore, when you order seed, state as accurately as possible the following data of future planting site: altitude; longitude; latitude; annual rainfall; length (and time of the year) of possible dry period(s); and any particular or extreme character of the soil (clay or sand; pH; salinity; slope; drainage; aspect). You may also state which other species are planted at or grow near the planting site. It is not realistic to procure seed particularly suited for all provided data, but the more information you are able to state, the more likely it will be that the supplier can provide seed that will develop successfully.

Seed quality

When we talk about the quality of the seed, we think of both physiological quality, which covers the state of health of the seed, and the genetic quality, which covers the properties that the seed has inherited from the parent trees.

The physiological quality of a seed is usually revealed in a germination test or a staining test with tetrazolium chloride. Both require laboratory facilities. To get an immediate idea of physiological quality, note these points:

a) The seeds should be clean (without dirt, leaves, twigs or fruit flesh)
b) There should be no insect holes or fungi
c) The seeds must appear intact and without cracks in the seed coat
d) The embryos should look firm and healthy

When seed is bought from seed dealers, results from germination tests, moisture contents and number of living seeds per kg should be documented. High moisture content in orthodox seed may indicate bad quality. It cannot be avoided that seed lots undergo some degree of deterioration during storage. Therefore young seed lots should preferably be chosen. In order to show the inherent/genetic qualities the seed must usually be grown into large plants or trees. It should be known what the trees are suited for; the home area (origin) of the parent trees should be known to make sure that seed source matches future planting site; it should be known what kind of mother stand the seed lot has been collected in, e.g. from many trees, from single or isolated trees, from a 'selected' stand with generally good looking and well growing trees or from a number of trees of mixed form and health. To have good genetic quality the seed lot should:

a) be suited for the purpose of tree planting
b) be suited for the planting site, i.e. come from a similar climate or have proven suitable under similar conditions
c) come from not less than 25-50 mother trees
d) come from average or better than average trees in a good stand. Crooked trees along roadsides may be of below average genetic quality and should in general not be used.

Cost of seed

A number of expenditures are necessary for establishing a tree stand. Of these the cost of the seed makes up only a very small amount, while the majority is made up by establishment, handling, testing and transportation. The difference in price between 'bad' and 'good' seed is usually of no significance for the total amount of establishment cost, whereas buying the cheapest seed, merely because it is cheap, may turn out to be very costly in the long run. Getting hold of the best possible seed is money well spent. The 'best' covers:

i. The most appropriate for the end use
ii. The best genetic quality
iii. The healthiest.

The price should also relate to the number of living seeds per kg. As mentioned above, seed lots inevitably undergo some degree of deterioration, which means that older seed lots of the same kind should usually be cheaper than younger ones (in spite of the fact that extra storage costs are involved).

Amount of seed

It may be difficult to estimate how much seed to order as seed weight and viability vary greatly. It may be easier to calculate how many seedlings/nursery plants one would like to end up with or how large an area the seed should be sufficient for. When the buyer informs the seed dealer of number of required seedlings or size of planting area, the seed dealer can calculate the necessary amount of seed based on seed purity, seed weight, expected loss in nursery and during transport, and expected amount for replacement in the field. If the seed is to be used for seed research, both seed weight and number of seeds needed should be stated. If you want to try out a species that has never been grown in your local area, it should be tested in a pilot planting first.

Seed handling

Seeds are living organisms and must be treated with care, otherwise they may suffer external or internal damage. The seed should not be thrown about or injured in any way, and it should be kept under appropriate conditions, that they are kept cool and dry. Orthodox seeds, e.g. seeds of pines and eucalypts, can be stored for years if they are dry and kept under cool conditions. For these seeds, a rule of thumb applies that the mean viability period of the seed will double each time storage temperature is lowered 5 degrees (between 50°C and 0°C) and each time moisture content is lowered 1 % (between 14 and 5 %). These seeds should be kept at minimum 15°C, at high humidity and with good aeration, as the seeds respire and need oxygen. Recalcitrant seeds should be sown as fast as possible after collection. Ask your seed supplier if any pretreatment before sowing is necessary and how the seeds should be stored. If you collect seeds yourself and cannot find information about storage conditions, you must make your own experiments to find out how the seeds should be handled.

Time of delivery

It is important that seedlings are transplanted into the field at the proper time of the year, mostly with regard to the rainy season(s). Therefore seed should be delivered in good time for the seed to be sown and to develop into plants of plantable size, which again means that seed should be ordered well in advance. Another reason for ordering well in advance is the better chance of the dealer having the wanted seed in stock. If seed is not immediately available, additional seed collection or seed purchase from other sources will be necessary. As most trees only bear fruit at certain times of the year, this may take many months. It may even take years as some tree species only have good fruit crops at years' intervals. So, in some cases it is quite reasonable to order seed several years in advance. For recalcitrant seed, which cannot be stored, it is particularly important to order well in advance as seed dealers do not have these in stock.

Restrictions

The quarantine authorities in your country may require an import permit for seed bought abroad. This should be applied for well in advance and sent to the seed supplier. There may also be restrictions on import of certain seed because of the risk of pest and diseases, which means that a phytosanitary certificate has to be acquired. For recalcitrant seed, it is particularly important to avoid delay in customs. Therefore check with the authorities which documents are needed for seed import. Questions of intellectual property rights, access to genetic resources and patenting have become issues of political importance at international level. In response to this, it is getting more and more common that a signed 'Material Transfer Agreement' (MTA) is required by the seed supplier. MTAs define future intellectual property rights or plant variety rights over the plant genetic resources. MTAs may take a variety of forms depending on the intentions of the seed supplier. As one extreme they may be designed to avoid future intellectual property rights over the material and as another extreme they may be designed to encourage patenting and describe how benefits from such actions should be divided. MTAs are commonly used both for commercial seed trade and for seed which is supplied for research purposes, and may as such cover both donor/ recipient and buyer/seller relationships.

Seed supplier

As you can understand from the above, it is of great importance to order your seed from a reliable seed dealer. To be able to identify the right seed dealer, contact your national or regional tree seed centre, who may be able to supply seed or have experience with local seed dealers; or go through 'Tree Seed Suppliers Directory' issued by ICRAF; also, seed dealers can be asked to send their catalogues, and those providing most information on the seed are usually the most serious ones. However, it is usually a good idea to seek the advice of colleagues or national seed-centre staff, who may know the seed dealers and have experienced how serious and reliable they are.

Documentation

The information may be important later; e.g. if a seed lot gives good results, more seed of the same kind may be ordered; and if the results are poor, it will be equally important to avoid ordering the same again. Also it is important to register the results of the treatment applied to the seed.

References

Astinet, H. 1961. Forest tree seed- specification of provenance. Saatgut-Wirtschaft. World Seed Campaign Edition, p. 34-36.

Austin, T. 1959. Seed supply in Norwegian forestry. 12th Int. Seed Testing Convention, Oslo.

Barner, H. 1958. Frøforsyning og Foraedling Seed supplies and breeding]. Dansk Skovforen. Tidsskr., 43 (1):1-84.

Bouvarel, P. 1958. Les dangers d'abatardissement des peuplements de grande valeur; mesures de conservation. Proc. 12th Congr. IUFRO, Oxford 1956, 1: 434-440.

Faulkner, R. & Matthews, J. D. 1961. The management of seed stands and seed orchards. Proc. Int. Seed Testing Assoc., 26 (3): 366-387.

Food And Agriculture Organization Of The United Nations. 1952. Exchange of forest seeds and plants. Report of the 6th Session Conf., FAO, 1951: 82-83, 171-175.

Food And Agriculture Organization Of The United Nations. 1961. Forest seed directory. Rome, FAO. For. Com. 1994 Seed manual. Procedures for seed collection, handling, storage, pur-chase and accounting. Forestry Commission, Hobart, Tasmania.

Georgia Crop Improvement Association. 1958. Certification standards for fores tree seed 1961 crop bullietien 5 p.

Gohran, V. 1962. Fortegnelse over Nogle Egnede Importområder for Skovfrø til Anvendelse i Dansk Skovbrug [List of some areas suitable for import of forest seed to be used in Denmark]. Dansk Skovforen. Tidsskr., 9: 401-427.

Hermann, R. & Astinet, H. 1961. Handbuch zum Gesetz über forstliches Saat- und Pflanzgut. Wirtschaft-und Forstverlag Euting K. G.

International Seed Testing Association. 1959. International rules for seed testing. Proc. Int. Seed Testing Assoc., 24 (3): 475-584.

International Seed Testing Association. 1962. Amendments to the international rules for seed testing. Proc. Int. Seed Testing Assoc., 27 (4): 1079-1096

ISAAC, L. A. 1960. Problems and proposals for international certification of tree seed origin and stand quality. Proc. 5th World For. Congr., Seattle, U.S.A., 2: 690-696.

Karki, L. 1961. Foundation for forest tree breeding. Activity in 1960. Helsinki. Koospol. 1961. Seed and Plants of forest tree species in Czechoslovakia. Koospol, Prague.

Langlet, O. 1936. Studien über die physiologische Variabilitat der Kiefer und deren Zusammenhang mit den Klima. Medd. statens Skagsförsöksanstalt, 29.

Langlet, O. 1945. Om förflyttning av barrträdsfrö vid skogsodling [On the movement of tree seeds in forest cultivation]. Svenska Sksgsv. Förens. Förlag, p. 21-32.

Langlet, O. 1957. Vidgade gränser for förflyttning av tallprovenienser till Skogsodlingeplatser i norra Sverige [Wider limits for moving pine provenances to forest sites in North Sweden]. Skogen, 44:319.

Langner, W. 1963. Consequences of the development of varieties in forestry. FAO/FORGEN, 63-8/5.

Larsen, R.T.F. 1960. The certification of forest tree seed in Britain. Proc. 5th World For. Congr., Seattle, U.S.A., 2: 708-710.

Macdonald, J. et al. 1957. Exotic forest trees in Britain. For. Comm. Bull. No. 30. London, H.M.S.O.

Rohmeder, E. 1960. Problems and proposals for an international seed certification scheme for forest seed . Proc. 5th World For. Congr., Seattle, U.S.A., 2: 685-690.

Rossmassler, W. 1961. Control of forest seed and plant material in Germany. Forstpflanzen-Forstsamen, 3/4:6-9.

Rudolf, P. O. 1963. Forest Tree Seed Certification Iin the United States and some proposals for uniformity. FAO/FORGEN, 63-8/3.

Rudolf PO. 1974. Tree-seed marketing controls. In: Schopmeyer CS, tech. coord. Agric. Handbk. 450. Washington, DC: USDA Forest Service: 153B166.

Tschermak, L. 1953. Zur Karte der Wuchsgebiete des Österreichischen waldes. Öst Vjschr. Forstw., 94 (1): 29-35.

Tyszkiewicz, S. 1950. The production of forest tree seed and planting stock in Poland. Schweiz. Z. Forstw., 101 (6): 282-295.

Vincent, G. 1958. Selection and transfer of varieties of forest trees. Sbornik Csl. Akad. Zemed, Ved. (Lesnictvi), 4 (5): 341-356.

Vloten, H. Van. 1957. The development and organisation of forest tree improvement in the Netherlands. Euphytica, 6: 14-17.

Wakely, P. C. et al. 1960. Minimum standards for progeny testing southern forest trees for seed certification purposes. Southern For. Exp. Sta. sponsored Publication No. 20. 20 p.

Index